Cry Bosnia

Refugee boy, Belgrade *June 1992*

CRY BOSNIA

Words & Pictures by
PAUL HARRIS

Foreword by
Kemal Kurspahić

Introduction by
David Rieff

INTERLINK BOOKS
An imprint of Interlink Publishing Group, Inc.
NEW YORK

First American edition published in 1996 by
INTERLINK BOOKS
An imprint of Interlink Publishing Group, Inc.
99 Seventh Avenue · Brooklyn, New York 11215

ISBN 1–56656–212–0

The author and publishers wish to thank the following for their generous assistance
without which this book would not have been possible:

Europapier, Vienna & Ljubljana
Gorenjski Tisk Printing & Publishing Company, Kranj, Slovenia

Frontispiece:
At a prisoner of war reception centre in Zagreb a woman seeks
news of her mising husband, *January 1992*

Cover design by Jasminko Arnautović, Tuzla, and Mark Blackadder, Edinburgh
Book design by Combined Arts, Edinburgh
Colour separations by Gorenjski Tisk Printing & Publishing Company
Paper supplied by Nordland Paper, Germany, and Europapier, Vienna & Ljubljana
Printed and bound in the Republic of Slovenia by Gorenjski Tisk

Acknowledgements

My thanks go to all those who have made *Cry Bosnia* possible: to publisher Stephanie Wolfe Murray for her consistent belief and encouragement; to my friend Igor Potocnik of Europapier, Ljubljana, Slovenia and Zagreb, Croatia, for his support both moral and tangible; and to the printers Gorenjski Tisk, Kranj, for their support.

A vast debt of gratitude is owed to Kemal Kurspahić and David Rieff who saw merit in the project and devoted their precious time to write the foreword and introduction. Special thanks are due to Jock Hayward, Scott Bowers, David Diehl, Linda Biggam and Richard Kolbert of Hand Associates, Interlink's West Coast representatives, for their generous offer to donate all their sales commission to "Cry Bosnia," a charity inspired and initiated by the publication of this book.

Portions of the text have previously appeared in *Scotland on Sunday*, *The Scotsman*, *The Daily Telegraph* and *Tageszeitung*. My thanks go to the editors of these newspapers.

And finally I extend my gratitude to the many people in Bosnia, indeed all over the former Yugoslavia, without whose friendship and co-operation little of this would have been possible.

Paul Harris
Whittingehame, Scotland
January 1996

The Former Yugoslavia

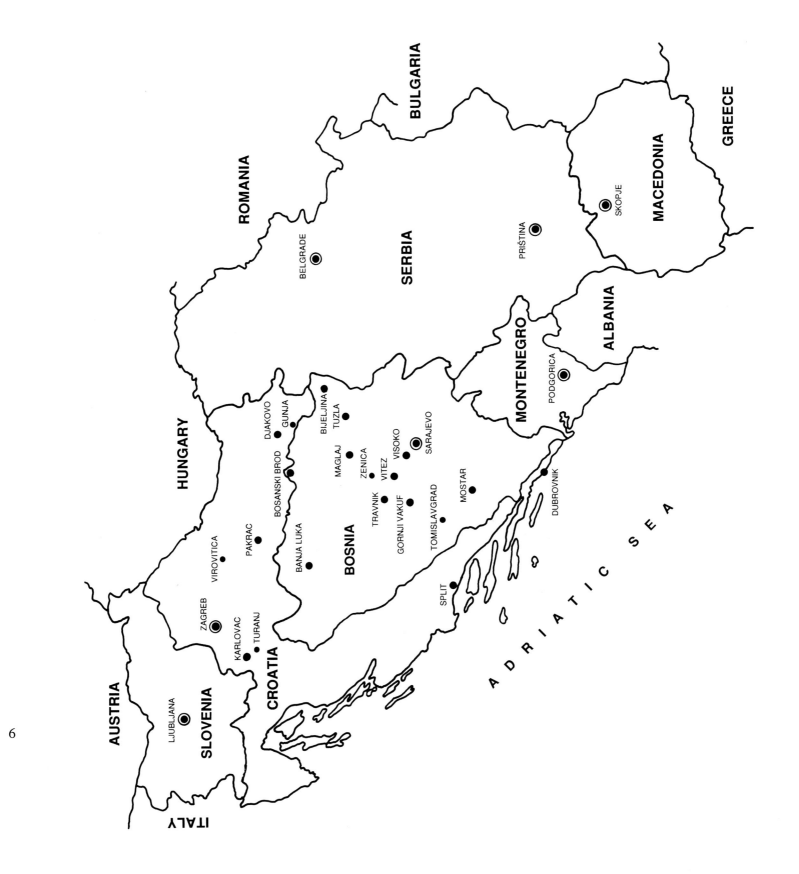

Contents

Acknowledgements   5
Map   6
List of U.S. Aid Organizations   8

Foreword by Kemal Kurspahić   9
Introduction by David Rieff   10
Preface   11

OVERTURE FOR BOSNIA *Don't They Know it's Christmas?*   17

RUMORS OF WAR *Namka's Story*   33

SARAJEVO *Survival in Two Movements*   49

CRADLE OF WAR *The Northern Corridor*   65

"WARRING PARTIES" *Bringing a Tear to the Eye of a War Criminal*   81

MOSTAR *Rebuilding Bridges*   97

THE REFUGEES *The Cleansed*   113

TUZLA *Putting it back together again*   129

Poems   142

U.S. Organizations Doing Humanitarian Assistance and Educational Work on Bosnia

AMERICAN FRIENDS SERVICE COMMITTEE
1501 Cherry Street, Philadelphia PA 19102
tel: 215) 241-7188 fax: 215) 241-7177
Relief project providing clothes and medical supplies

AMNESTY INTERNATIONAL
322 Eighth Avenue, New York NY 10001
tel: 212) 633-4200 fax: 212) 627-1451
Human rights monitoring and advocacy

AMERICAN JEWISH JOINT DISTRIBUTION COMMITTEE
711 Third Avenue, 10th floor, New York NY 10017
tel: 212) 687-6200
Rescue operations, food and medical aid, communications

AMERICAN RED CROSS
P.O. Box 37243, Washington DC 20013
tel: 202) 639-3906
Work includes medical and relief assistance, monitoring civilian population and detainees

AMERICAN REFUGEE COMMITTEE
2344 Nicollet Avenue #350, Minneapolis MN 55404
tel: 612) 872-7060
Food, medical aid, reconstruction and rehabilitation projects

CAMPAIGN FOR PEACE AND DEMOCRACY
P.O. Box 1640, Cathedral Station, New York NY 10025
tel: 212) 666-5924 fax: 212) 662-5892
Educational work, public forums on U.S. Bosnia policy

CARE
660 First Avenue, New York NY 10016
tel: 212) 686-3110
Food, shelter and infant support supplies

CATHOLIC RELIEF SERVICES
209 West Fayette Street, Baltimore MD 21201
tel: 410) 625-2220
Food, medical and seed aid, job creation, orphan care

CENTER FOR CONSTITUTIONAL RIGHTS
666 Broadway, New York NY 10014
tel: 212) 614-6464 fax: 212) 614-6499
Legal challenges on behalf of victims of war crimes

CHURCH WORLD SERVICE
P.O. Box 968, Elkhart IN 46515
tel: 219) 264-3102
Food and seed assistance, women's development projects

DELPHI INTERNATIONAL
1090 Vermont Avenue NW, 7th floor, Washington DC 20005
tel: 202) 898-0950
Technical assistance for women's organizations in conflict resolution

FELLOWSHIP OF RECONCILIATION
PO Box 271, Nyack NY 10960
tel: 914) 358-4601 fax: 212) 358-4924
Finds U.S. scholarships and host families for Bosnian students

HUMAN RIGHTS WATCH
485 Fifth Ave, New York NY 10017
tel: 212) 972-8400 fax: 212) 972-0905
Monitoring, issuing reports and human rights advocacy

IMMIGRATION AND REFUGEE SERVICES OF AMERICA
1717 Massachusetts Avenue NW #701, Washington DC 20036
tel: 202) 347-3507
Mental health and social service programs for refugee youth

INTERACTION: American Council for Voluntary International Action
1717 Massachusetts Ave., NW, #601, Washington DC 20036
tel: 202) 667-8227 fax: 202) 667-8236
e-mail:ia@interaction.org
Network of humanitarian assistance organizations

INTERNATIONAL MEDICAL CORPS
12233 W. Olympic Blvd., #280, Los Angeles CA 90064
tel: 310) 826-7800
Provides new ambulances and trains doctors in trauma care, children's health program

INTERNATIONAL RESCUE COMMITTEE
122 East 42nd Street, 12th floor, New York NY 10168
tel: 212) 551-3061
Food and agricultural assistance to refugees, mental health program for women and children

ISLAMIC AFRICAN RELIEF AGENCY/USA
P.O. Box 7084, Columbia MO 65205
tel: 314) 443-0166
Food and medical relief, hospital intensive care unit, orphan sponsorship program

LUTHERAN WORLD RELIEF
390 Park Avenue South, New York NY 10016
tel: 212) 532-6350
Emergency food, housing, clothing and construciton aid

MADRE
121 West 27 Street, #301, New York NY 10001
tel: 212) 627-0444 fax: 212) 675-3704
Support for women rape victims

MEDECINS SANS FRONTIERS USA (Doctors Without Borders)
30 Rockefeller Plaza #5425, New York NY 10112
tel: 212) 649-5961
Medical aid and monitoring, water provisions

OPERATION USA
8320 Melrose Avenue, #200, Los Angeles CA 90069
tel: 213) 658-8876
Medical and hospital supplies, medical/surgical training team

PHYSICIANS FOR HUMAN RIGHTS
100 Boylston Street, #702, Boston MA 02116
tel: 617) 695-0041 fax: 617) 695-0307
Collects forensic evidence for International War Crimes Tribunal

SAVE THE CHILDREN
54 Wilton Road, Westport CT 06880
tel: 203) 221-4100
Educational/psychological assistance for refugee families

UNITED METHODIST COMMITTEE ON RELIEF
475 Riverside Drive, #1374, New York NY 10115
tel: 212) 870-3816
Reconstruction, social services, emergency food

US COMMITTEE FOR UNICEF
333 East 38 Street, New York NY 10016
tel: 212) 686-5522
Special focus on children's programs

WORLD VISION RELIEF AND DEVELOPMENT
919 West Huntington Drive, Monrovia CA 91016
tel: 818) 357-7979
Cash, food, clothing, medical assistance

Foreword

by Kemal Kurspahić*

One of the most shocking experiences during all those long months of the Serbian siege of Sarajevo was that of watching the international community ignore the crisis. People trapped in the Bosnian capital, running for their lives in a cruel Serbian version of Russian roulette, were targeted by snipers or mortars while waiting for bread, water and humanitarian aid distribution, deprived of the most basic necessities, of water, electricity, heating, gas, telephone lines. Their children were massacred while sledding or attending improvised schools. They were exposed to endless terror and humiliation – and could not believe that all those ideas of a New World Order, all those "never again" promises, all those international authorities like the UN, Europe, the US, NATO and all the others, were not going to do anything to stop the strangulation of the city. The siege lasted even longer than the historic assault on Leningrad.

The international community, used the United Nations to hide its refusal to respond and its self-imposed impotence, behind the all-excusing claim of "neutrality."

"We are there to keep the peace, not to make war; we have to be neutral." became the litany of UN peacekeepers to explain the total failure of their mission. In fact there was no peace to keep and they were not neutral; through the arms embargo they kept Bosnia's hands tied in the face of brutal military force. Relying on that sick idea of "neutrality" between victims and victimizers, they abandoned their mandate to protect "safe zones" in Bosnia, resulting in thousands of civilians in Srebrenica being slaughtered by the Serb forces practically in the presence of UN soldiers. The Western powers allowed heavy weapons within the "exclusion zone" around Sarajevo to be fired at the city from collections points under the direct supervision of UN troops. And they obscured their fear of getting involved, and confused the international public with platitudes about how "those people have been killing each other for hundreds of years," even after the CIA reported that at least 90 per cent of the genocidal crimes of "ethnic cleansing" were committed by the Serb forces, and even after the UN Commission of Experts on War Crimes concluded that "there was no factual grounds for moral equivalence" in the responsibility for those crimes.

In the post-Cold War vacuum of leadership, in the absence of international understanding that Yugoslavia's communism had been replaced by the racist ultra-national forces of "ethnic purity," in the unwillingness of the international leaders of the 1990s to take the risks of confronting genocide – in the face of all of this it was the international media which alerted the public, moved legislatures, woke up humanity.

Without Roy Gutman's stories on the Bosnian Serbs' death camps in the summer of 1992 many more people, hundreds or thousands of them, would now be "missing" like those thousands of men from Srebrenica slaughtered by Serb rebels in 1995. Without the heroic reporting of journalists like Maggie O'Kane or Ed Vulliamy, the British public would have been much more easily manipulated by Lord Owen-like politicians who were spreading equal blame "on all sides of the conflict." Without the cries for humanity of French intellectuals like Bernard-Henri Levy, who knows whether French President Chirac would have taken the lead in confronting Serb aggression in the summer of 1995.

Paul Harris, with this moving collection of photographs and notes from the Balkan war zones, from Vukovar to Sarajevo all the way to Mostar, joins those brave and highly professional journalists who took the risks to witness and to document the genocide. This book is his certificate for a place among those who give honor and integrity to their profession.

* Kemal Kurspahić is former Editor-in-Chief of the Bosnian daily *Oslobodjenje* (published daily in Sarajevo throughout the siege). He was named International Editor of the Year in 1993.

Introduction

by David Rieff*

The facts about what happened in Bosnia are simple enough, for all the mystifications that have been built up around them by politicians looking for an excuse not to act and by ordinary people looking for an excuse not to care. Bosnia was never about ancient ethnic hatreds, ancestral blood feuds, or the innate savagery of the Balkans rising from the ashes of Titoism. In other words, though it may be more consoling to believe the contrary, Bosnia did not commit suicide; it was murdered. The architect of the assassination was the former Communist party boss of Serbia, Slobodan Milosević who saw in Great Serb nationalism the ideal vehicle for holding on to power. The accomplices to the murder are too numerous to mention but they include, alas, all the great powers of the Western world who declined to act and instead stood by as for the fourth time in a century, a small European minority was marked for extermination.

The Armenians, the Gypsies, the Jews, and now the Bosnian Muslims. And this in Europe, the continent that had proclaimed itself, over the course of the last half century, to have put such savageries behind it forever. Such are the ironies of history that at the moment that President Clinton was dedicating a museum to the Jewish holocaust, another genocide was taking place in the hills of Bosnia. And two years later, in the summer of 1995, as much of Western Europe and North America celebrated the fiftieth anniversary of the victory over fascism in World War II, the *entire* population of males aged twelve to sixty in the Bosnian government-controlled enclave of Srebrenica that had not managed to escape when the Bosnian Serbs overran their town were separated, just as at the railhead at Auschwitz half a century earlier, and marched off for execution.

Marek Edelman, the last surviving commander of the Warsaw Ghetto uprising has remarked that the victory of Great Serb nationalism in Bosnia represents the posthumous victory of Adolph Hitler. He has the right to say such things. Those of us who do not can still insist that for people of conscience alive today, the shame of Bosnia will be something they will live with for the rest of their lives. Shame about what it says about our "civilized" societies, obviously. But also shame about what it reveals about the relationship between knowing about a horror and doing something about it. For unlike the Armenians, the Jews, and the Gypsies, the Bosnian Muslims were killed, raped, and evicted from their lands "live" on the nightly news. The press at great risk – 48 foreign journalists were killed covering the Bosnian war, and several hundred were wounded – managed to expose what was going on. Reporters chronicled the Serb concentration camps in northern Bosnia, lived through the siege of Sarajevo and the destruction of East Mostar, and rode the aid convoys across the confrontation lines. The photojournalists in particular like Paul Harris took the lion's share of the risks and did the most to make the Bosnian tragedy real to a world that didn't want to listen. But the politicians back home had already made up their minds to let Bosnia die.

As Harris himself points out bitterly – and it is a feeling all of us who covered the Bosnian war share – no one will be able to ask, as they did after Auschwitz, "'why were we not told.' Well, the world *has* been told." Harris' book, *Cry Bosnia*, is one, especially eloquent rendering of the story. But it does not only tell, and lament, it also asks the question that the foreign press corps in Bosnia, supposedly so hard-bitten, has been asking in one form or another since the beginning of the slaughter: "Why did so few care?"

On one level, the answer is obvious. It was a faraway conflict – from America at least, though not from Europe – taking place in a selfish time. The help that has finally come has come too late to save the Bosnia that existed before 1992. But what the press tried to convey was a truth that shouts from every page of *Cry Bosnia*: Our failure to help not only condemned the Bosnian Muslims to their fate, it also constituted a moral death sentence on our own societies. So when we weep for them, we should really be weeping for ourselves.

* David Rieff is an American journalist who lived in Bosnia on and off between 1992 and 1994. He is the author of *Slaughterhouse: Bosnia and the Failure of the West* (Simon and Schuster, 1995).

Preface

Cry Bosnia

It is Easter. The second weekend in April, 1992. In the village of Gunja, on the borders of Croatia and Bosnia, the president of the local community asks when the West will help. He may well ask. The local school where we are sitting is packed with refugees; and they are not the loincloth variety. Recently dispossessed from neat, well-ordered modern homes, many have chosen to flee in their best suits. One girl, tottering on high heels, simply observes, "If I had to leave my home with nothing, then at least I was going to leave wearing my best shoes."

In the three days that I have been in Gunja I estimate that more than 10,000 refugees have poured over a narrow wooden footbridge suspended on scaffolding poles over the River Sava. They are coming from all around the Bosnian town of Brčko, on the other side of the river. True, all hell might be breaking loose in the capital Sarajevo, but, in northern Bosnia, just a few days into what will become a devastating war, it is already crystal clear, here on the ground, that Serb forces are in an advanced stage of redrawing the map of a vast swathe of the country.

I had a strong feeling that I was witnessing some sort of turning point in the tide of human affairs. At the time, I wasn't aware of the immense significance of what I was witnessing that weekend, although I did write: "This was a mass human exodus of vast proportions ..." I asked myself if I was not going over the top. But it sounded good. It also actually turned out to be all too true.

Sometimes the things you witness are, self-evidently, important. The Yugoslav Federal Air Force Super Galeb was returning to base. The wreckage of civil aircraft at Ljubljana's Brnik Airport – including the Airbus A230 on which I was supposed to fly that day – was being doused around me. I knew this was *the* turning point in June 1991 – as Belgrade mobilised its armed forces against fellow Yugoslavs. But so many incidents, so many individual events seem, somehow, ordinary at the time. Even though they are, by any normal set of standards, quite extraordinary.

Almost a year later I remember driving through northern Bosnia. At the time I simply did not understand what I was seeing. All around, on both sides of the road, houses were burning yet no shells or rockets were landing in the area. As I got closer to the river crossing point at Bosanski Brod, I could see men emerging from normal, modern family homes with empty plastic containers in their hands. Then another house would go up in flames. At this early stage in the Bosnian war, the two words had not yet come into currency. What I was witnessing, although I did not know it at the time, was ethnic cleansing.

It is May 1992 and in a farmhouse kitchen a few kilometres outside the northern Bosnian city of Modriča the women of the house, grandmother, mother and daughter, are serving up a meal – in much the same way as they must have done for the men of the house for generations. The steaming goulash is delicious, the hospitality impeccable. An everyday, timeless scenario in Bosnia. Except for the constant – as yet distant – '*booom*' of heavy artillery as Muslim and Serb fight for control of Modrica: within the month the Serbs will have taken this entire region, including the farmhouse in Pečnik. Over lunch, I am politely asked when the West will help ... I have by now grown used to demurring helplessly at this question. In truth, I am embarrassed by it. In time I will get over my embarrassment but I will still feel accountable and guilty whenever the question is raised over the next three years or so.

As I write this, in the summer of 1995, the question is no longer asked. It is accepted that the West will not come to the rescue of Bosnia. A young soldier at the military headquarters of the government 3rd Korpus in Zenica realistically, rather than cynically, observed, "Where were you when we needed you? It does not matter now. *Now we will finish this thing ourselves.*"

It is pointless to try and explain to people who are dispossessed, starving, under fire, or whatever, that long distance TV observers in the West are inertia-bound, do not understand this foreign conflict and above all simply do not want to get involved. At the sharp end of the frontline, so to speak, imperatives are immediate.

Here it is impossible to explain the conceptual basis of western policy. Well, you see, something new has to happen around here for Bosnia to get up the TV news agenda. Something rather dramatic, really, and it would be awfully helpful if CNN happen to be around. Yes, the market place massacre in Sarajevo, 68 dead by a single mortar impact, is the sort of thing that gets people wound up – and makes the politicians pursue some new initiative. No, another market place massacre wouldn't really be good enough. It would just be a re-run of the same story. And the May 1995 shell into Tuzla with 72 dead was not quite in the right place. CNN wasn't there and the Serbs were taking UN hostages. Something different is needed …

All this sounds pathetically unprincipled to a soldier on the frontline; a civilian cowering in a basement; or a refugee living under canvas because he or she has lost literally everything in the world.

In an outstanding and emotive *Panorama* broadcast in January 1993, Martin Bell tried to destructuralise the myths and cut through the largely imagined complexities. Western intervention was at that time very much the issue. He put the argument powerfully and movingly. "The case for intervention is not to help one side against the other, but the weak against the strong, the unarmed against the armed; to champion the everyday victims of war … It is fundamentally a question of whether we care."

But the story of Europe's, America's and the West's mishandling of the Yugoslav crises has consistently been one of too little too late. This is not an epitaph hopefully, but certainly the story so far. It is of Europe's and America's prevarication and an unwillingness to commit. It seems barely credible today, that in the summer of 1991, US Secretary of State James Baker was affirming in Belgrade that Yugoslavia must stay together as one state and further, that this view represented the cornerstone of US policy in the region. You wonder just *who* was advising the White House. Any reasonably experienced Balkan watcher could have warned of the dark forces that would be unleashed by this green light to Serbia, even if the 'spooks' at Langley, Virginia could not.

As a direct result of Baker's insouciance, Belgrade, in the form of Serbian nationalist President Slobodan Milosević, was encouraged to go to war: firstly against the tiny Republic of Slovenia and, when that proved a surprisingly inept and unsuccessful effort, within the month against Croatia. With the notable exception of Germany, Europe and America affected not to recognise the political realities and held out against recognition of either state until January 15, 1992, prolonging those first phases of the war and encouraging its spread, by the beginning of April, to Bosnia.

Initially, economic sanctions were applied indiscriminately against the whole of former Yugoslavia before being applied specifically to Serbia and its ally Montenegro. The arms embargo on all states of former Yugoslavia remained in place and – grotesquely unfair – has been applied to embattled Bosnia as much as to Serbia. That embargo is a matter of some indifference anyway as far as the Serbs are concerned. Before the fighting broke out, Yugoslavia was a net exporter of armaments and conservative estimates at the time the arms embargo was imposed indicated that Serbia had enough weapons and munitions to fight on for more than ten years.

Lord Carrington was fond of citing the apparent willingness of the so-called 'warring parties' to carry on fighting as some sort of rationale for standing back from the conflict. I recall sheltering in a bar in the Croatian town of Vinkovci in October of 1991 as the shells fell all around. On the TV in the corner of the noisy bar, Carrington pontificated about 'knocking heads together in the Balkans' as if we were all on the playing fields of Eton. I was surprised they couldn't hear the jeers in Brussels or New York.

Even if the fighters were determined to carry on, that could be no principled reason for the abandonment of hundreds of thousands of quite innocent civilians. The UN became involved, initially, in Croatia following a peace accord which came into effect in January 1992. With quite extraordinary imprescience, the headquarters of the UN operation in Croatia – the United Nations Protection Force (UNPROFOR) – was established far away in volatile Sarajevo as the war clouds gathered. The mandate was then extended when war followed in Bosnia: to secure safe deliveries of aid to hundreds of embattled communities. This operation soon became particularly vital in the besieged enclaves and in Sarajevo, as a sophisticated modern society was suddenly and brutally thrust back into the Dark Ages with a swiftness which was scarcely credible, even to those observing events at close hand.

The material damage which followed can scarcely be imagined: it is possible to drive for twenty or thirty kilometres in some places and not see an undamaged building: the financial cost of this damage may, at some later stage, be calculated. The human cost of a continuing, largely unchecked campaign of ethnic cleansing is, as yet, quite incalculable and the full implications for Europe of a vast rootless refugee population will possibly not be assessed before the end of this century. Even the TV *reportage* fails to capture the all encompassing tragedy, so enured to the most disturbing of TV images have viewers become.

That having been said, public shifts in policy by politicians have tended to follow the more disturbing TV images. The screening of the after effects of the mortaring of the bread queue in Sarajevo on May 27 1992 led to sanctions against Serbia within days; the mortaring of the market place in February 1994 led to almost a year of peace in the city as the UN, at least for a while, threatened to take on the Serbs with NATO jets. And, in May 1995, when worldwide TV audiences were treated to the unedifying sight of UN personnel chained to ammunition bunkers and airfield installations in the baking sun, the UN at last put together plans for a rapid reaction force to tame the Serbs.

Now, I am afraid I am altogether too cynical to believe that the actual showing of these horrors was any sort of revelation to the politicians who, in turn, instituted action: the machinery must already have been in place. What was awaited was a suitably horrific occurrence to force that retaliatory action.

The press and TV reports of the death camps in northern Bosnia shocked the viewing and reading public all over the world. But it would be naive to assume it shocked their political leaders. In a world where aerial surveillance means that an AWACS aircraft can spot you putting a letter in the postbox at the end of the road, it is reasonable to assume that the politicians in London, Washington, or wherever, had, for months, been pouring over the photographs of death camps, wondering just how to present this to their electorates, and assessing the political downside these inconvenient misfortunes might present.

This serves to highlight just what a spineless lack of moral leadership has been displayed by political leaders on both sides of the Atlantic. The Balkan conflict, in large part, has been dismissed as 'somebody else's war'. To paraphrase Chamberlain, it has been perceived as a war in a faraway country involving people of whom we know little – and care less. In this attitude, political 'leaders' have done not just the Bosnians, not just Europe, but also their own electorate a profound and quite immoral disservice. It is, surely, no coincidence that some of

the most effective and ambitious aid efforts in Bosnia have been those of small charities and private individuals and organisations, operating outside 'official' governmental channels. Ordinary mortals have tended to rise to the challenges presented by the Bosnian crisis where their 'leaders' have been conspicuously absent.

Of course the appeal for some sort of pro-active interventionist policy, made with such force and clarity by Martin Bell, went the same way as the millions of words written by other journalists; the miles of videotape shot by TV cameramen; and the tens of thousands of rolls of film shot by photographers: into some great void. *Plus ça change.* Martha Gellhorn, veteran of more than a dozen wars, observed in the introduction to her own collected writings, *The Face of War*, "For all the good our articles did, they might have been written in invisible ink, printed on leaves, and loosed to the wind."

For every journalist who has been asked by a soldier, civilian or refugee if the cavalry will ever come over the hill, there is a journalist who seeks the way to express more effectively the reality of what has been happening in Bosnia: to seek to create a form of words or a sequence of images which might have some effect.

Are you naive to think there might be some cumulative effect, some sudden breakthrough, to justify all that film and tape, all those words and images, all that intrusion on the grief and suffering of others? Naive, possibly, but without that hope, however faint, it would seem pointless to carry on. Equally, if the story had never been told there can be little doubt the horrors and carnage would have been incalculably worse. And, decades later, there would justifiably be the accusations, the insinuations, the suspicions. 'Why were we not told?'

Well, the world *has* been told of the Bosnian conflict, in graphic detail and in thousands of images. From the bread queue massacre of May 1992 through to the market place massacre of February 1994 by way of ethnic cleansing; rape camps; concentration camps; investigations of the war crimes tribunals; the unrelieved medieval-style siege of Sarajevo; the plight of the enclaves of Srebrenica, Zepa, Bihać and Gorazde; the destruction of Mostar, one of Europe's most beautiful medieval cities; the continued ritual humiliation of United Nations forces; failed cease-fires and 'peace processes'; So many stories, so much blood, so much tragedy unfolded, layer upon layer, before the reader and viewer. In ever increasing – and ever more apparently acceptable quantities. Just like pornography.

Of course, journalists and TV people are fairly hard-bitten. But, this time around, perhaps their own universal outrage stems not so much from their *temoinage* as from the realisation of the ineffectiveness of their own leaders: the duplicity, the deviousness and the shameless Machiavellian manipulation of the lives of people evidently perceived, in domestic electoral terms, as being expendable.

The first significant public evidence of a new element of determination in US policy came in March 1994 when President Clinton brought President Izetbegović from Sarajevo and President Tudjman from Zagreb to sign up for a new Bosnian-Croat federation after a year of bitter fighting between Croats and Muslims in Bosnia. US involvement had thus far been limited to a broad policy of containment – the placement of 1,000 US soldiers on the Macedonian side of the Serbian border, and support for the Albanian government and armed forces in a bid to prevent 'overspill' of war.

By the beginning of 1994, however, the warning signals at the White House were too insistent to ignore. For a start, the impact of the television images from CNN and other American networks now regularly covering the conflict was of increasing concern. Bosnia was producing too many irregular and unpleasant surprises. Most alarmingly, the CIA predictions were dire. If unchecked, the war would spread through the Balkans and ultimately involve NATO allies Greece and Turkey in taking sides with the protagonists. A UN withdrawal in disarray from the region looked to be inevitable, followed shortly thereafter by the effective collapse of NATO. Even from the distance of the White House lawn, this prospect was altogether too bleak to contemplate.

US strategists and policymakers correctly identified the fact that the virtually unchecked, and continuing, advance of the Serbs had to be halted. To that end, the warring Croats and Muslims had to be brought together as allies once again. Support for the Muslim-Croat federation was the more public part of the policy. Then, at the beginning of September 1994 a top level US delegation secretly visited Bosnia.

The turning point came in the central Bosnian town of Gornji Vakuf early in the afternoon of Sunday, September 4. Flanked by US Special Forces men in dark glasses, four star USAF General 'Chuck' Boyd strode alertly down the shattered main street in his neatly pressed flying suit taking in the roofless homes and the walls pockmarked by bullets. In his wake came a trio of three star generals and a couple of civilians – the US Ambassador in Sarajevo, Victor Jakovec, and a large bespectacled man in shirtsleeves who I did not recognise. "Who's that?" I asked Brig. Gen. Mike Hayden, on the basis that as Head of Intelligence, US European Command, he should know.

"That's a guy called Richard Holbrooke. He's some new Special Ambassador." On a street corner in Gornji Vakuf, Boyd and Holbrooke quizzed local army commanders. They reached differing conclusions. Holbrooke came away convinced that the US should involve itself more actively in Bosnia. Boyd was less sanguine. He came to the conclusion that NATO and the US should not become involved militarily. He wrote, in an article published in the influential *Foreign Affairs* after his retiral as Deputy C-in-C US European Command in July 1995, "At the end of the day the United States must face the reality that it cannot produce an *enduring* solution with military force – air or ground – only one that will last until it departs."

Unlike Boyd, Holbrooke was prepared to utilise diplomatic guile, bullying and subterfuge and he recommended a multi-layered approach subsequently adopted. Whilst he started on the diplomatic offensive, which built up to his frenetic shuttle diplomacy of the summer and autumn of 1995, a programme of covert US assistance to the Bosnian and Croatian governments was launched.

US Special Forces helped build an airstrip capable of taking heavy transport aircraft for the Bosnian government in a secure location in a valley near to Kakanj in central Bosnia. 'Logistics advisers' moved into key locations throughout Bosnia, including the UN-controlled airbase at Tuzla Airport – which is now to be the headquarters for US troops in Bosnia. Airdrops of weapons and supplies were made by Hercules C-130 aircraft to the remoter landing strips at Tuzla at a time when a Jane's Defence Information Group editor noted C-130s at US bases in Germany with their markings painted out. US-operated AWACS aircraft failed to report movements back to NATO on the nights in question and UN statements about US involvement issued in February of this year were hurriedly withdrawn after "incandescent" US intelligence personnel descended on UNPROFOR headquarters in Zagreb. A Virginia-based 'private company', Military Professional Resources Inc., became military advisers to the Croatian armed forces and masterminded this year's successful Operation

Storm which drove the Serbs out of Croatia's occupied Krajina territory in textbook operation curiously redolent of NATO manuals. Then, of course, the head of MPRI was newly retired NATO military chief General John Galvin . . .

All this covert activity ultimately ended with the NATO bombings of key Serb positions in August 1995 – and the apparently unilateral US attack on Banja Luka's command and control systems with Cruise missiles at the beginning of September. This, like the attack by US aircraft on Krajina's Udbina airbase on the morning of August 4, the first day of Croatia's *Operation Storm*, perfectly paved the way for the underdogs – the Muslim-Croat alliance – to level the so-called playing field. In turn, the levelling enabled the Croats and Muslims to retake territory approximately in line with the Contact Group maps for a 51% federation split as against 49% to be held by the Serbs. The Serbs were thereby forcefully convinced of their sharply deteriorating military position.

Whilst openly professing the virtues of peace, President Clinton and his advisers had, in fact, taken on board the inescapable fact of life in the Balkans. Might is right and the force of military arms was what would ultimately bring the parties to the table.

By the beginning of December 1995 advance parties of US troops were in position in Bosnia readying their new HQ at Tuzla airbase in the north of the country, and just a few days before Christmas the might of the US Army's 1st Armoured Division started its move-in from Germany.

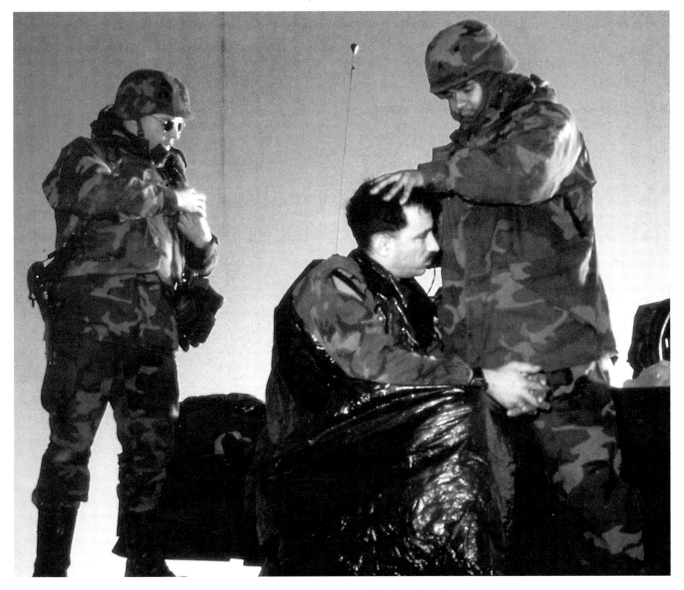

Newly arrived American soldiers from the 1st Armoured Brigade of 1st Armoured Division, one of whom is having his hair cut. Županja, Croatia, *Christmas 1995*

American soldiers readying themselves for their peacekeeping role
in Bosnia on an Abrams M1A1 tank. Županja, Croatia, *Christmas 1995*

Overture for Bosnia

Don't They Know it's Christmas?

It is the season of goodwill to all men and a small Christmas tree illuminates the bleak corridor outside the mortuary at Djakovo Hospital, just a few kilometres from Croatia's eastern frontline.

The bodies of the three Croatian National Guardsmen were brought in around mid-day on stretchers and laid out in the white-tiled room for post-mortem. Still dressed in their dark green camouflage uniforms, their features were frozen as if at the moment of death. The yellowed pallor and the staring expressions – of seeming disbelief at their fate – lent them the appearance of skilfully executed waxworks. But waxworks they were not. Brutal execution was what had cut short their lives but a few hours previously.

Their features aged in death, these three young men were just 23, 25 and 28 years old. They had lived in the same village of Sodolovci; they had all been friends and they had joined up together three months previously to protect their village from the Serbian irregulars, the Chetniks, who had started to infiltrate the area. With the fall of Vukovar, the front line gradually edged nearer and nearer to their village and the fighting was suddenly all around: reaching the beleaguered towns of nearby Vinkovci and Osijek.

The previous night the three had set off from their village on a night patrol. When they had not returned by dawn, search parties were sent out. Villagers combing the woods discovered their bodies in a shallow grave. It was evident they had been shot but the full horror of their death was only to become apparent with the post-mortem.

Their commanding officer arrived. Solidly built, self-assured, you could sense he was a leader of men. No time was wasted, he had done this before. Deftly, he emptied the pockets; useful items of equipment were retrieved for future use; documents and papers laid aside. Then the bodies were stripped. This was heavy work. *Rigor mortis* had set in and the bodies had to be cumbersomely manhandled by the officer and two surprisingly young female doctors.

Soon the manner of their death became apparent. All had been shot: many times in both arms, but these wounds were not the cause of death. Their bodies had been cut with knives and then two had been finished off with knife wounds to the heart. The third had died when his head was battered and crushed, most probably with a rifle butt.

Dr Jelko Milić, head of surgery at Djakovo Hospital, was in no doubt about the sequence of the night's events. "These men were taken prisoner. Some of the wounds may have come in the fight but they were shot in the arms later, tortured and then killed."

The door to the mortuary was opened to let in the cold, fresh air and to dispel the rising stench. Every so often, the young girls would go out into the fresh air in their bloodied white overalls, wipe their brows, gulp down the clean air, and then return to their grim work.

The soldiers standing around the door are transfixed by the horror. Nobody notices a little old man making his way to the open door. He looks old; very old. Old enough to have seen three of these wars. His face is deeply wrinkled and weather-beaten, the face of a man who has worked his life on the land. His jacket, probably his best, is a couple of sizes too big and flaps around. Too late the soldiers see him but he is too quick. Lowering his head, he weaves between them like a hare in flight and then is at the mortuary door, peering in at a vision of hell. There is silence for a brief moment as he takes in the scene and then a desperate, piercing wail. "Mou sin, Mou sin." *My son, my son.*

Led gently from the mortuary, he breaks free from the soldiers and, clutching his head in his hands, he runs to and fro, hither and thither, wailing piteously. Tears are now running in rivulets down those aged wrinkles on his face. He is inconsolable. All attempts at comfort are shrugged away.

Other relatives arrive. One young wife collapses at the door of the mortuary and is carried away by two soldiers. The doctors carry on with their gruesome work. And, all the while, the old man continues his anguished dash around the outside of the mortuary building.

Half an hour or so later, I prepare to leave. The

doctors are wiping the blood from the white-tiled walls. Dr Milić sucks pensively on a gold cigarette holder. "Yes, I am a professional and I have seen this before. But it is still very difficult for me." There are tears in the eyes of a soldier standing at the door. The commanding officer makes unrepeatable observations about the Chetniks. And the old man continues his anguished progress, repeating over and over again in frenzied disbelief those same two words. "Mou sin! Mou sin!"

In themselves, casualty figures convey little. They are but cold statistics despite their apparent scale. Before that Christmas, the unofficial death toll in Croatia was estimated at between six and ten thousand dead. Even then, I reckoned it might probably be nearer 20,000 when all the shallow graves had been emptied, and all the rubble of the hundreds of devastated villages had been sifted. By way of example, it was an open secret in Zagreb the week before Christmas that there had just been a terrible and tragic reverse in this war. Near to the village of Pokupsko, just 28 kilometres from the capital, an attempted Croatian offensive had gone horribly wrong. Hundreds of young soldiers of but a few weeks training, in reality engineers, teachers, lawyers and clerks, had been forced back to the banks of the fast flowing River Kupa. There, in the terror of flight, they drowned in the river.

The disaster was not admitted to by the Ministry of Information: they said two men died. A soldier who was there said 490. And at lunch in Zagreb those around the table knew half a dozen who had died there.

Remote from such horrors, it is difficult enough to appreciate the deep wounds left on all the living who will mourn 490 men, let alone the 10,000, the 20,000, or whatever, who have died in just six months of conflict. It is difficult to adequately convey the scale of the tragedy in bald statistics.

There is, however, one simple uncluttered image which does convey it all in microcosm. An image which conveys more than all the casualty figures.

That image of an old, old man, his head in his hands, running around the mortuary building at

Inside the Church of the Holy Trinity, Karlovac, Christmas Eve. The Christmas tree goes up and the stained glass windows are protected by sandbags. *December 1991*

18

Djakavo locked in his own frenzy of personal despair.

It must have been a bitter Christmas in Sodolovci. In the silences between the singing and the prayers you could hear the impatient chatter of machine gun fire outside; the explosion of mortars; and the dull crump of heavy artillery. The singing was loud and passionate, as if in direct defiance of the incessant reminder of the horrors being enacted outside the Franciscan Church of the Holy Trinity in the town of Karlovac. This was the reality of a mist-laden, drizzly Christmas Day in Croatia, 1991.

The assembled worshippers must, superficially at least, have resembled any congregation elsewhere in Europe that Christmas morning. Sprucely turned out children, their cheeks reddened by the sub-zero temperatures outside; peasant women and widows in black; townswomen in their furs and hats; old men in their best suits. But, as you looked around that packed church a few minutes before morning mass was due to begin, there were no young men, few fathers and certainly no men of military age. Then, just as the service was about to begin, men in uniform filtered in through the congregation. They came in twos and threes until the church was packed. There they stood crowded into the nave in their green camouflage uniforms, heads bowed and hands crossed respectfully. Here and there were the German-made dark brown uniforms of the 110th Brigade, which included the foreigners who have come to fight here, and Serbs who had elected to stay and fight with the Croatians. And, in stark contrast, conspicuous in its pristine white, was the uniform of a solitary EC monitor.

At the end of the nave, where you would normally have been able to see the ornamental stained glass in all its glory, sandbags were piled to the roof. The frontline is only three kilometres or so from this 17th century church with its painted frescoes, finely wrought pews and its prized black Madonna. The 80,000 inhabitants of Karlovac had been under daily bombardment since September 15. Whether or not by Divine intervention, this beautiful church had thus far been spared, but all those gathered there must have been aware of its fragility, its awful vulnerability in the face of devastating modern weapons of war.

Even for an outsider, uninvolved in the day to day traumas of this war-torn community, the service was a deeply moving experience. Prayers for Croatia, prayers for their own community, prayers for the soldiers, prayers for the bereaved and prayers for the dead. Even a prayer for the journalists killed in the war. And for the EC monitors.

Some of the women cried. But as I looked around, it was clear that most of the soft, gentle sobbing was coming from the soldiers. From the men in uniform, none of whom could have been soldiers for any more than six months, and who had seen so much in such a short time. I had only once before seen the faces of men like that – two days previously at that mortuary in Djkakovo. And I knew why these men were crying.

Christmas lunch had not been on the menu when I set out that morning but it unexpectedly appeared when I arrived at military headquarters in Karlovac to collect a military escort to the frontline. In the mess, soup, chicken and vegetables, salad and cake, were all washed down by an excellent Dalmatian wine.

A couple of kilometres up the road in the village of Turanj, just across the river from Karlovac, they were also lunching, and fighting, when we arrived in the afternoon. A couple of tank crews, clearly expecting not to do any business that day, were singing noisily in the kitchen of a farmhouse, an empty bottle of Kentucky whisky on the table. In a stone barn across the road a hot Christmas meal was being delivered to the couple of dozen or so soldiers billeted there.

I had last been in Turanj in the middle of September and had sat outside on the terrace of a neat cafe in the warm autumn sunshine. That same cafe, like all the buildings around, was now totally devastated: its roof blown in, its interior gutted by fire, the outside pockmarked by bullets and the striped awnings hanging down in shreds. Some wag had crudely painted the legend *Hotel California* on a piece of charred wood. This village was now the

EC Monitor Eric Gautier, Turanj, Christmas Day. *December 1991*

killing ground with just two or three hundred metres dividing Serb and Croat. Nobody now lived in this once prosperous village, lately full of people who went to work in the textile factories and engineering works of Karlovac. Within sight of Turanj is the Jugoturbina works. In June it employed 10,000 people. Today, I am told, after three months of wilful damage, there are just 200 workers.

There is a heavy, damp mist. For this we are grateful. It cuts down the sniper activity and observers can't call in the mortars. The mud lies thick and glutinous as we pick our way gingerly through shrapnel, shell casings and the detritus of war. A shell lands noisily a couple of hundred yards or so up the road setting light to a once neat, whitewashed house. We take cover in the barn where Christmas dinner is being devoured. The soldiers sleep here in shifts before moving up the road to do battle. In the corner is a Christmas tree complete with decoration and lights – the only light in the room – next to a radio operator intercepting morse messages in the gloom.

One of their number has been killed a few hours previously in the yard outside by a mortar bomb and they have just finished burying him. Nevertheless, morale seems remarkably good. Or at least there is much bravado about. A young soldier approaches and touches my arm.

As I look into his eyes, I know that I am looking into the face of a deeply troubled man. Jadranko is 21. He speaks perfect English and he desperately wants to talk. Conscripted into the army just a few weeks previously, he had finished three years of a five year course in shipbuilding engineering. "I know I must fight for Croatia. But really I want to learn. To live." I recognise that he is looking for some reassurance from me; that he instinctively feels I will understand his unhappiness and fear. But our talk is interrupted by the guffaws of his fellows who are, I realise, poking fun at him. The commanding officer waves me away from him, lest I become contaminated. Jadranko slinks away into the darkness of a corner, retreating into his own misery, the weakest animal in the pack.

Christmas Day brings Turanj its own footnote in the history books. The very last convoy of Federal troops to retreat from Croatian territory under the supervision of EC monitors leaves here mid-afternoon to cross over into Bosnia, just three kilometres down the road. This rearguard is made up of the mine disposal team and their equipment from Pleso barracks, near Zagreb. They remained behind to try and clear the mines from around the barracks. The problem was they laid the mines without charting them and so three of their number died trying to locate them in the frosty ground of winter.

Passing the convoy through the lines turns out to be a tricky operation. Although only a few hundred metres separate the two sides, communication is currently only being conducted through the barrel of a gun. My respect for the European Community (EC) efforts improves dramatically when the white jeep with its blue insignia simply drives up the road into the mist, its klaxon hooting noisily. It comes under fire and after a couple of minutes turns back. One of the monitors points out to the Croatians that they have failed to remove all the mines – there are still deadly Saracen anti-personnel mines on the road. The Croatians give the distinct impression they aren't really that bothered.

The French leader of the EC team, Eric Gautier, rounds on them and addresses them like so many naughty children. "Right, I tell you what I am going to do. I am going back up that road and I will stand beside those mines and wave the convoy around."

And that is precisely what he did. He had guts that Frenchman. That was the only truly Christian act I witnessed in Karlovac that Christmas Day. But why did he do it? Not for Croatia, not for the retreating Serbs. Certainly not for Europe. I think I know why. He was that EC man bowed in prayer in the Church of the Holy Trinity on Christmas morning.

20

Yugoslavia is unravelling. In Ljubljana's main square, the flag of a newly independent Slovenia is planted in the bronzed hand of the statue of the poet, writer and national hero France Preseren. *June 1991*

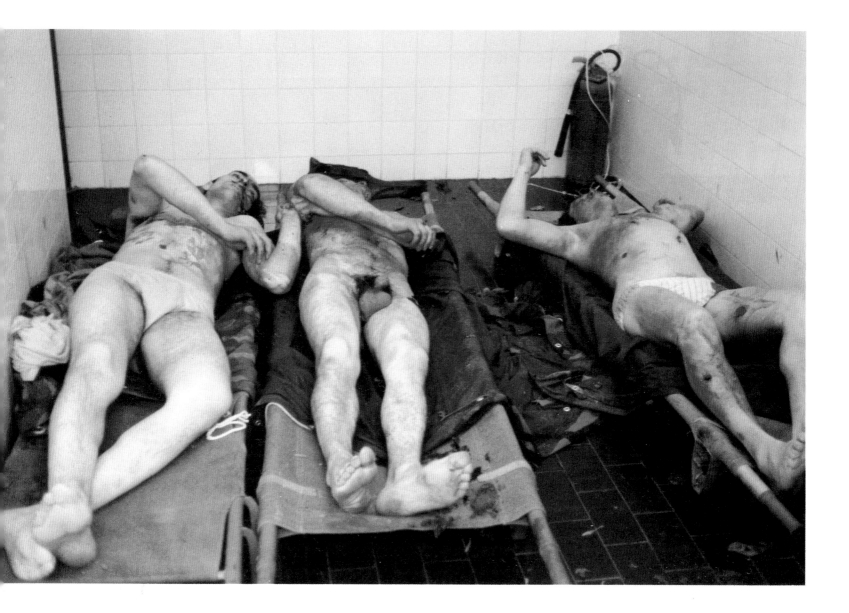

Images of Christmas Eve in Croatia. In the late morning they were bringing the bodies into the mortuary at Djakovo Hospital (*top left*). The lights of the Christmas tree in the corridor shone bleakly into the white-tiled mortuary as the bodies were stripped and examined before postmortem.

Around one o'clock a young woman arrived in a car with two Croatian army officers (*above*). Inside is the body of her husband lying on one of the stretchers. He has been tortured and then killed. She collapses.

Eight hours later in the capital Zagreb (*bottom left*) you might hardly realise a war is being ruthlessly prosecuted all around, save for the camouflage uniforms in the bars and discotheques. These two girls had come here for a night on the town, travelling from the once industrial, now frontline, town of Karlovac – just 40 minutes drive away down the motorway. They just want to forget the war. Over Christmas, Karlovac was shelled unremittingly by the besieging Serbs.
December 24 1991

Rozika Militić, the battling granny of the village of Kamenica, became something of a legend after she and her sons and grandsons captured a Serbian tank, then sent to military headquarters in Karlovac for a manual, and turned it against their attackers. She commanded the tank whilst her progeny drove it and operated its weaponry.

Alas, the day I visited snow-covered Kamenica it was not in action. The battery was flat – but Rozika was in good spirits. *February 1992*

25

"Everything is gone." I photographed this Croatian woman in the tiny village of Plostice, on the road to besieged Pakrac, in the early days of war: she was, in fact, the first war refugee I had ever encountered. At the time, this woman in the back of a horse drawn cart was a curiosity: it was as if she had stepped straight from some book or film. A peasant woman, she had lost everything – farm, animals and home. At that time I had no background against which to place her, no perspective in which to see her. All her energy and pent-up emotion suggested to me that I was about to witness something quite beyond my ken, but, as yet, I had actually seen nothing of the damage and brutalisation of war. *September 1991*

Just two months or so into the war in Croatia, the town of Pakrac, in Western Slavonia, was already divided between local Serbs and Croats. Federal forces of the Yugoslav army and air force were attacking the Croatian fighters with artillery, aircraft and mortars. The local fighters – boys in jeans and trainers with antique weaponry uncovered from barns and attics – came to the fight with quite extraordinary enthusiasm. Here I was waved on into Pakrac by Danijel. A few months later I heard he was shot in the heart. I often wonder what became of him and his friends in the village of Prekopakrac. *September 1991*

Above. The photograph of the little girl whose bedroom this once was still sits on the wall inside her shattered home, silent testimony to the speed and ferocity with which war overtook the village of Turanj, right on the demarcation line between the Croatian forces and the breakaway Serbs of Krajina. In September of 1991 this was a neat and ordered village across the river from the industrial town of Karlovac. By Christmas, not a single house stood undamaged. *December 1991*

Top right. Little Alen has lost his parents in the maelstrom of war. They are now missing behind the lines in part of Eastern Slavonia taken by the Serbs. In the childrens' hospital in Zagreb the four-year-old is an abandoned piece of the flotsam of war. The doctors are apologetic about him: he is offered a cuddly toy every day but he prefers his life-size Kalashnikov replica and stubbornly fights off all attempts to remove it. *November 1991*

Bottom right: Zagreb *November 1991*

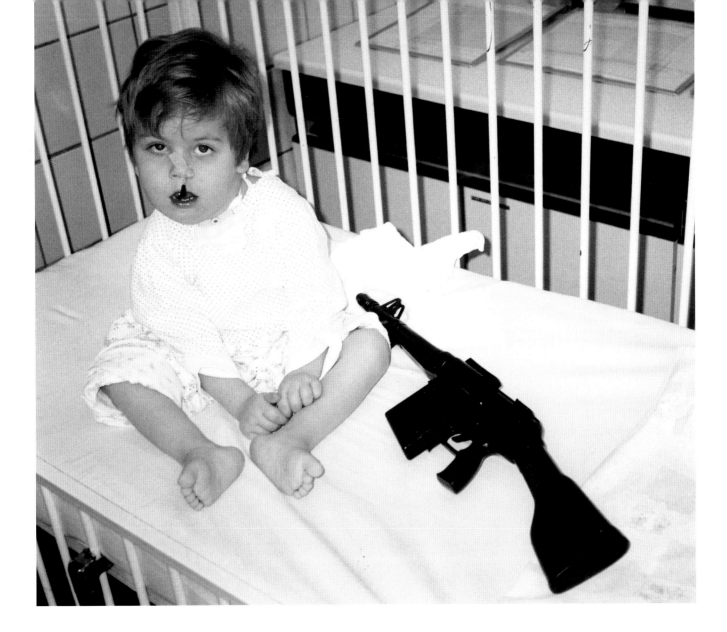

Left: The railway children. Six-year-old Anton is one of the railway children. He told me he used to live in a nice house with a garden in the eastern part of Croatia but now, along with two hundred other refugees, he shares a railway carriage as a home. Ironically, just ten kilometres up the road from the siding at Klanjec is the birthplace of the architect of post-war Yugoslavia, Josip Broz Tito. *February 1992*

Above: In peasant communities the links between people and livestock are not just close but, rather, immutable. This woman abandoned all her possessions and fled with her cattle. *October 1991*

31

At a prisoner of war reception centre in Zagreb, relatives of the missing wait anxiously to see if their own loved ones are on the lists of those newly released. For most there is no news. It will be more than a year before news starts to emerge of the massacres which followed the fall of Vukovar and other towns and villages in Eastern Slavonia. *January 1992*

Rumours of War

Namka's Story

It is the period between Christmas and New Year. The period when most Europeans are recovering from the excesses of Christmas and looking forward to the promise of an approaching new year. In Travnik, the ancient Turkish capital of central Bosnia, the prospect of a New Year was one of uncertainty and trepidation.

The scene is the refugee centre. It is in the middle of a frontline town under constant, though unpredictable, shell and mortar fire. A single mortar drops just down the street, seemingly from nowhere, just as mortars are prone to do around here. For the 500 or so refugees packed into the former schoolrooms of the town's secondary school, this is, I suppose, a haven of sorts. Here they eat, sleep and live, as many as thirty to a room: in the gymnasium there are more than 100. There are no sanitary facilities in the old school, although outside a team of irrepressibly cheerful cockney workers from the British construction group Bovis – funded by the Overseas Development Agency (ODA) – are erecting toilet and washing facilities in prefabricated units. These are desperately needed and not just to alleviate patent discomfort. Typhoid is in danger of becoming endemic in the refugee centre.

It was not as cold as you would expect at this time of year inside the vast lofty corridors and classrooms of this school erected by the Austro-Hungarian rulers of Bosnia just over 100 years ago. Over Christmas, it was only around minus ten at night in the unheated rooms. It was to get colder. And the bitter cold serves to drastically reduce the refugees' resistance to disease.

There are no young men amongst these predominantly Muslim refugees. There are mothers and children. There are old people. Sons and brothers, husbands and lovers are dead, fighting or simply missing in the whirlpool of war.

There are two beds forming an island in the middle of one schoolroom. A paltry few possessions are spread out on the bed. Clothes hang drying against a wall. All around, traditionally dressed Muslim women and a few elderly men sit in a limbo of enforced idleness. The middle of this room is home for a 35 year-old woman, Namka, and her four children. This is their story as told to me by Namka through my interpreter. Present at the interview was the director of the centre, my interpreter and a BBC cameraman. The elemental power of her deeply moving account is best conveyed in her own words. This is Namka's story of a night of terror.

"My name is Namka Hedis and I lived in the village of Hadzici near to the town of Prijedor (in northern Bosnia about 25 miles from Banja Luka). The Chetniks (Serbian irregular troops) came to our village in trucks at 5 p.m. on June 20th. They came to our house and ordered my husband, Racib, his four brothers and his father to stand at the front of our house. My husband was 37 years-old and had just returned to the village from his work in Slovenia. I was ordered to bring the children outside. We were made to watch as they first shot my husband, then the others, with pistols.

"Then one of the Chetniks put a knife to my throat and pointed at my children, Emin (14), Emina (11), Ernest (7) and Anita (4). 'Choose which one of your children is to die. You must give us one of them.' I could not choose but they took hold of the youngest, Anita, who is just four years old and held their knives to her throat. I thought they would kill her. In the confusion we were all screaming and crying." (Anita was not killed. Other horrors take over.)

"All the men in the village were killed. There were three thousand men in the area and many were executed that night. Then they started to rape the women – mainly the younger women. But the oldest woman I saw raped was 70 years old. The youngest was 12. Many of the women who were raped had their throats cut afterwards. I don't know how I survived.

"At the end they took our money and our gold and our Serbian neighbours told those of us who had survived to leave the village. We walked to Travnik (almost 120 kilometres) only with what we could carry."

Namka thinks all of her relatives are now dead.

Her parents lived in the village of Bosanski Novi. It is known that the people there met a similar fate and her parents are not registered at any of the refugee camps.

I ask if she might return to her village if the Serb advance is ever rolled back. "It is difficult to say what we might do. But I think there are now too many terrible memories in our old village." Namka had no way of knowing what 1993 might hold. Her only horizon was the cell-like window of the room in the refugee centre they dare not leave for fear of shell and mortar. One day in November, refugees taking the fresh air in the streets outside the centre were raked by anti-aircraft fire directed downwards from the mountains above Travnik.

As she recalls the horrors of that Breughel-like night of medieval hell in central Europe of 1992, I am, successively, incredulous, then horribly fascinated, gradually moved and, ultimately, helplessly enraged that such things can happen little more than two hours flying time from London, Paris or Berlin.

The older children have not lost their animation and still smile for visiting strangers. But all the while, as this woman grown old beyond her years but not shorn of dignity by her experiences, bravely tells her story, her four year old daughter sits listlessly on her

Namka and her daughter, Anita, at the refugee centre in Travnik. *December 1992*

knee, eyes unseeing, registering no feelings or reactions to any of the activity in the room around her. This is puzzling. The TV camera at least can normally be relied upon to produce a reaction in even the most traumatised of children.

But Anita does not speak any longer. She has not spoken a word since the evening of the 20th of June. Since the night she saw her father murdered before her and the men with big beards and funny hats held their knives to her young throat.

I had found Namka's story so harrowing that I suppose I was loathe to believe it. Although I had written her story and believed the tale of how she and her children were forced to witness the execution of her husband and his four brothers, the mass rapes, the pillaging, the looting and the destruction of their homes, I somehow found it beyond comprehension that such things could happen.

I had to find the village of Hadzici. Not so much because I doubted the sincerity of her story as I doubted my own understanding, my own conception of what could actually have happened during the night of June 20. Despite the evidence of my own notes, the *témoinage* of my interpreter and the TV camera which recorded the interview, this was something so inexplicably awful that, having learned of it, I had to get closer to in order to comprehend.

And so my interpreter and I passed through the UN controlled 'pink' zone of central Croatia, across one of the two remaining bridges over the River Sava at Bosanska Gradiska and into northern Bosnia: into the so-called Serbian Republic of Bosnia, or Srpska as it was termed. We drove for four hours or so along the deserted roads: there were almost as many horses and carts on these roads as cars, with working filling stations as much as 100 miles apart.

Roadblocks and checkpoints were many and unpredictable, but our UN accreditation worked successfully for us. At one checkpoint my electric razor was seized on by an officer who went through every bag and crevice of the car. He was deeply suspicious of what was evidently a mysterious object until one of his men showed him how to switch it on. He almost jumped out of his skin. You may not be quite back in the middle ages but in some of these remote parts the time warp stretches back at least half a century.

I knew the approximate location of Hadzici and we searched until nightfall. I am baffled: the names of towns and villages on the map do not match those on the signs. I start to doubt my own map reading and we press on through the night to our next destination.

In Knin, the capital of the Serbian Republic of Krajina, Serb-held Croatia, one hundred and fifty kilometres to the south, the press centre is located in the military headquarters. Conveniently on the wall on the first floor is an enormous large scale map of Krajina, northern Bosnia and Croatia. A military map, it is the best I have seen and I am able to plot the position of Hadzici precisely. Checking the map against my notes, it is only then I realise that the more overtly Muslim sounding names of villages and small towns no longer exist on the ground. The places may remain but the names have been changed.

We leave at dawn the next morning and head back through the mountains into northern Bosnia. We pass through Titov Drvar, where Tito hid in a cave from the 1943 attack by elite German parachute troops. The cave was once a national shrine: it is now closed up. Then through the town of Bosanski Petrovać and down into a valley at the village of Bravsko. A few houses at the side of the road are destroyed but what may have overtaken them is, thus far, unclear. We are now in the village of Velagici and I know from the military map that the next must be Hadzici.

We pass over the crest of a hill and Hadzici stretches before us to the right of the road. The location is one of almost breathtaking beauty. In the sun, the frost-covered slopes of the valley stretch gently down to the road and the streets and houses of the village are stepped in layers on the hillside. It is a sizeable village, really almost a town, and you can imagine it as a place of bustle and trade. There any illusion stops.

We are looking at a panorama of devastation. Modern and traditional family homes alike lie gutted and blackened. I recognise immediately the evidence of ethnic cleansing. Houses destroyed by shellfire bear quite different trademarks: holes in roofs and walls, the distinctive cartwheel impressions of the mortar or the pockmarked impressions of flying metal. But here, virtually every house, maybe as many as four or five hundred, is totally destroyed by fire as far as the eye can see. Abandoned looted possessions litter once neat gardens, strips of stained curtain flap from broken windows and black smoke marks streak their way up to the very tops of the white painted walls. Roof timbers have been consumed by fire and red tiles litter the interiors and gardens.

No longer do I need to struggle to imagine the armageddon which overtook Hadzici. I have heard it from Namka's lips and now I can see the evidence with my own eyes. Narrative and reality blend together in the most terrifyingly complete of images.

Set on its own below the village and close to the road was the mosque. The shattered pencil tower of the minaret still stands above the wreckage of the walls, collapsed in on each other, the largely intact domes untidily stacked on top of the debris. Again, this strong modern structure was not destroyed by a shell. It was blown up with dynamite.

There is a checkpoint ahead and I snatch some photographs through the car window before we are upon it. We draw to a halt with packs of Marlborough to hand: cigarettes are necessary currency in these parts. These are gratefully received and we are cleared to proceed. We ask what could have happened here, pointing at the evidence of devastation. "The Croatians destroyed the village," one soldier asserts. I suggest that, therefore, we should take photographs as evidence of this appalling destruction. "Nema slikka. Nema slikka." Photographs are absolutely forbidden.

A little further down the road we give a lift to an unshaven and surly young lad in a cobbled-together uniform and dirty boots. He smells strongly of drink. He is training as a policeman. He is slightly more accurate, if understated, in his interpretation of what has happened here. "The Muslims were complaining." He uses the Serbo-Croat word *bunili* which translates less literally as "giving us a bad time".

He goes on, "So one night they went away." Just like that.

On the fringe of the village, a horse and cart is emerging driven by a middle aged man and his wife. No couple could look more harmless. Presumably, two of Namka's Serbian neighbours still eking out their lives amidst the ruins. Our passenger opines unprompted, "We Serbs can't hate, you know. It's not in our nature. We are simply defending what is ours."

We pass the new signboard for the village. Pud Hanin, it announces. Not only has a whole way of life in Hadzici been extinguished in one night of brutal mediaeval madness, but all evidence of Namka's village has been erased.

The flight from Bosnia begins. At the beginning of April the ethnic cleansing of northern and eastern Bosnia began as Serbian forces started to clear Muslims and Croats from villages earmarked as ethnically Serb. This was happening even before the siege of Sarajevo started. Most of the bridges across the River Sava linking Bosnia and Croatia were blown up for military-strategic reasons, like this bridge which connected the northern Bosnian town of Brčko to the village community of Gunja in Croatia. A precarious and narrow walkway was constructed using scaffolding poles and wooden planks. Over the Easter weekend I watched more than 10,000 people flee across this improvised escape route. *April 1992*

Most of those who fled over the bridge at Gunja from their villages in northern Bosnia escaped with little more than they could carry in a few pathetic plastic bags. Their faces said it all. As yet, the world did not realise what was happening in Bosnia. The traffic here was almost entirely one way: women and children fleeing death and persecution. Then, once every hour, the traffic was briefly halted as men, returning from their jobs in Europe, filed across into Bosnia to fight for their homeland.

At the end of April, the footbridge was blown up by Serbian fighters early one morning, pitching all those on the bridge to their deaths in the river below.
April 1992

40   A timeless image. Not Warsaw 1939, but Gunja 1992. *April 1992*

Over Easter weekend hundreds of Bosnians fled across the fast flowing waters of the Sava in small boats, arriving at an improvised landing point by the Croatian village of Babena Greda. Amidst the black-clothed peasant women, one smartly dressed figure stood out. A young girl called Olga (*left*), she had arrived home at her village in northern Bosnia

on Good Friday from her job in Germany. As she sat down with her family for dinner, their Serbian neighbours arrived at the door and gave them ten minutes to leave their home. The women fled; her father and brothers stayed to fight. That weekend, Olga stood on the Croatian side of the river staring across towards her village and wondering if she would ever see them again. Outside northern Bosnia, nobody, as yet, had any conception of the horrors being enacted. *April 1992*

44   Flight across the Sava. *April 1992*

Temporary refuge. These young men have fled from northern Bosnia into Croatia as non-Serbs were driven out of their villages. Those deemed to be of fighting age were sent back to Bosnia by the Croatian army and police. The youth whose papers are being examined was duly sent back to fight. *April 1992*

45

Burning house near Odzak, northern Bosnia. I was puzzled when I saw this house burning. No shells appeared to be landing in the vicinity. I was travelling alone and I stopped and approached the building which was well alight; all around there were other homes which were either on fire or smoking. Even more puzzling, I could see police and military vehicles in the area. Their occupants seemed oblivious to the burning homes. The phrase was unknown at that time – the Bosnian war had only just started – but what I was, in fact, seeing was ethnic cleansing at work. In retrospect, it was unwise to stop and take the pictures. But I knew not what I was witnessing. *May 1992*

46

By the time I took this photograph, I knew well what had happened. Namka Hedis had told me in graphic detail about that night of terror in her village of Hadzici in June 1992. I set out to find her village, in Serb occupied northern Bosnia. This was the mosque in Hadzici. It was evident it had been blown up with explosives. Photographing it was something of a problem. The evidence of this wanton destruction was sandwiched between two military checkpoints, just a few hundred metres apart. All photographs in the area were forbidden. I took a series of photographs with a small compact camera held inside my jacket as the car passed the ruins. Just one successfully captured the scene.
February 1993

I visited the town of Bosanski Brod several times at the beginning of the Bosnian conflict. The first time was in February 1992 as the referendum on the future of Bosnia was held. It was unseasonably warm and sunny and the pavement cafes were already full. On the outskirts of Bosanski Brod, armed Serb fighters had erected road blocks to disrupt the referendum and renamed the area 'The Autonomous Serbian Republic of Bosanski Brod'. This was where the fighting in Bosnia really started.

Within six weeks, the centre of the town was devastated, civilians were underground and only newly enlisted soldiery cruised the streets. There was still an enthusiasm for war, undented by military failure. *April 1992*

Sarajevo

Survival in Two Movements

After a year of unrelenting horror and tragedy the beleaguered citizens of Sarajevo have become accustomed to the bizarre. Even the most emotionally jaded could not fail to be moved as two musicians took up position in the middle of the devastated amphitheatre of the Skenderija Youth Centre, once home to rock concerts, dances and, in 1984, the medal presentation ceremonies for the Winter Olympics. In white tie and tails, with the sound of shell and mortar resonating all around, they serenaded a group of Sarajevo artists and writers. The Serb snipers perched in their front line positions just 150 metres or so away.

For cellist Vedran Smailović this was no new experience: he has been defying the snipers with his cello for almost a year. But for the viola player, Nigel Osborne, composer and Reid Professor of Music at the University of Edinburgh, this was something without equal in his career. As they moved through last Tuesday's repertoire, Nigel Osborne's specially composed *Adagio for Smailovic*, Albinone's *Adagio*, Greig's *Solvaig's Song* and Paul Macartney's *Yesterday,* they drew in the infuriated fire of the Serb snipers. Against a dramatic backdrop of smoke-blackened concrete, charred wood and twisted metal, the two black-coated figures played in the very centre of the snow covered arena, their audience sheltering amidst the ruins of the stadium.

But this was more than a defiant statement directed at the besieging Serbs, it was also the establishment of a tangible link between Sarajevo and Edinburgh. For 44-year-old Osborne, prominent Bosnian activist and one of the organisers of the Sarajevo-Edinburgh initiative, dedicated to the establishment of links between the artistic communities of the two capitals, this was the performance of his life: the incontrovertible physical evidence of his commitment. "I had to go to Sarajevo to establish my personal contact with the situation. A sort of personal moral frontier I had to pass."

In Sarajevo, no one man symbolises the spiritual defiance of the city more than the popular 38 year-old Vedran Smailović. This effusive, heavily mustachioed, larger than life, six-times-married cellist with the Sarajevo Opera started to play in public in the most dangerous of places after the bread queue massacre in May 1992, when more than 20 men, women and children died in a horrific mortar attack. In the frontlines, in the exposed graveyards and in the parks of the city, he mournfully played out Albione's *Adagio for the Dead*. He played for 29 days in one place. On the thirtieth he had a bad feeling in the morning: when he passed later that afternoon there was the blood of another in the very place where he normally sat. A mortar had fallen just two metres from his normal place.

On another occasion he had a telephone call in the morning. "This is Milan, your old Serbian neighbour now up in the hills above Sarajevo. Do not return to the graveyard today. Today the snipers will take you. This is the last warning I can give you."

For Vedran, his cello is his personal weapon. He really believes he can bewitch his potential attackers with its mellow tones and, in this way, he literally charms them from the trees. "When I'm playing, I'm already in heaven." He believes he can create his own protective aura: so far, it has worked but as we sneaked our way through narrow streets and alleyways, I found myself unwilling to place too much trust in his luck. As Vedran walked defiantly in the middle of the streets, I hugged the sides and took advantage of such cover as offered itself. Nigel followed, also visibly less certain, clutching his borrowed viola. And the flak-jacketed and helmeted Francis Best and her German Vox-TV crew covering the event followed behind in their specially armoured, bullet proof Audi.

Nigel is wearing the tailcoat of the Serbian violinist Kamenko Ostojić. The string quartet of the Sarajevo Opera is now a duet: two of its members have died in the attacks on the city and Nigel today temporarily replaces Vedran's fallen Serbian colleague. The Edinburgh academic and composer, trained in Oxford and Warsaw, imbued with what he terms 'Eastern European modernism' and possibly better known in Eastern Europe than in Britain, has the firmest of views on the retention of the multi-ethnic and multi-cultural structure of

49

Bosnian society. He wears Ostojic's morning dress with a particular pride.

Vedran's playing is deep and contemplative. He plays with a special kind of heavy passion. The siege of Sarajevo has liberated extremes in his performance style. Also, at a more physical level, he has lost some of the mobility in his fingers in the cold of this long winter without heating: a winter in which he has been unable to practise properly.

Finding a drink in Sarajevo can be difficult these days but Vedran has a nose for such necessities of life. The public water supply has broken down completely in the face of unremitting Serb attacks on basic utilities. In the Cafe Ragusa we relax over a rare glass of red wine ($100 a bottle) and the deliciously cool water from the melted snow, collected in buckets from the leaking gutters at the back of the building. For Zlatko Hadzidedić the morning's concert was significant in its own special way: poet and playwright, he was picked up in the street a few weeks previously and forcibly taken to dig trenches for the Bosnian army at the frontline positions where we have been today. On a loudspeaker in the background Roy Orbison poignantly intones *Everything you Want*.

All this may seem but a minor blip in an unremitting landscape of war. But as Miro Purivatra, the director of the internationally respected Obala Theatre of Sarajevo, put it that week, "All this is absolutely vital to maintain our mental health. For us, at this time, it is far more important than food parcels."

In a high-ceilinged, cold rehearsal room in Sarajevo's National Theatre the singers wear hats and coats. Their breath is expelled in great white clouds in the unheated room. Through the bullet holes in the glass of the 100 year-old Austro-Hungarian building the minus eight degree cold steals in from the street. The building has been hit by no less than

Sarajevo was a cosmopolitan European city of domes, minarets and tower blocks. View from the Turkish fort above the city. *February 1995*

43 shells: nobody knows, or bothers to count, how many bullet holes. High up on the wall a photograph of Marshall Tito still stares benignly down on a city which refuses to abandon his multi-ethnic and multi-cultural vision of Yugoslavia.

At the grand piano a huddled group is gathered to rehearse the brand new operetta *Europe*: composer Nigel Osborne; Sarajevo writer and poet Goran Simic; director Dino Mustafic; and beautiful red-haired rock singer Amila Glamocak, cast in the role of 'Miss Europe'. You get the impression that a sort of minor miracle is in process.

It is Wednesday. Osborne has been in Sarajevo since the previous Saturday. When he arrived on a Hercules C-130 UNHCR transport aircraft, with the partly written score of his *Europe* tucked inside his flak jacket, it was to the news that a space had yet to be found for the opening event of Sarajevo's Winter Festival. But Sarajevo is the city where all things are possible. By Tuesday, Ibrahim Spahić, director of the ten year-old Winter Festival started in the wake of the Winter Olympics of 1984, had secured the use of the National Theatre, The Sarajevo Philharmonic Orchestra and one of the city's most outstanding directors.

Osborne has fitted well into Sarajevo in the course of his half dozen or so visits. A tireless worker for Bosnia through a string of charities, he is at once dogged and determined and a patient, charming diplomat, qualities which might reasonably be regarded as *de rigueur* for anyone venturing here. The story of the ship 'Europa' is a metaphor for what is happening in the Balkans and in Europe. It is a tale which will surely go down well around here.

The director, Dino Mustafić, is a worried man. "This is impossible," he mutters, "We have just one week for everything. For rehearsals of singers and orchestra, for scenery, for lighting, for Nigel to finish composing this opera." Bespectacled Osborne beams genially through his beard. "After this, Dino, we will all be in *The Guinness Book of Records*." You get the impression Dino is neither *au fait* with, nor concerned about, the cataloguing of bizarre world records, although he has himself pulled off some outstanding directorial feats in war-torn Sarajevo, including productions of Sartre's *The Wall* and Ionesco's *Rhinoceros*. At a local level, these are quite on a par with the better publicised achievements of American director Susan Sontag who has been here to produce *Waiting for Godot*.

Entering through the stage door is an immediate and noisy challenge in the form of a 120-strong choir-come-dancing troupe of Sarajevo children.

These are the *palćići*, literally translated, 'the little thumbs'. This bubbly group, every one a would-be star, has to be tamed and trained. This job falls to Toby Gough and Roxana Pope, from the International Foundation for Training in the Arts (IFTA), and who have been organising drama workshops all over Bosnia at the suggestion of the charity Scottish European Aid. The duo have come to Sarajevo by way of Tuzla in the north of the country, recruited by Osborne both for the opera and to start off a series of drama and music workshops in Sarajevo.

"We're not really supposed to be here," Rocky bubbles. "We don't have UN accreditation." Every foreigner around here generally has an UNPROFOR card. "We came into Sarajevo through the tunnel under the airport with the Mayor of Tuzla who kept whispering *Don't speak English, don't speak English*". Peace may for the moment have broken out in Sarajevo but the city is still as firmly as ever under siege by the Serbs, with only two ways in and out: by UNHCR aid flight, for which UN credentials are required, or by a low, narrow tunnel – a former drainage channel – under the airport and which is strictly for the use of locals, in much the same way as the flights are for foreigners.

The two energetic young people seem to be able to relate to the children – with just a little rudimentary Bosnian – in the secret way that drama teachers seem able to dispense with normal communications forms. Toby has three Edinburgh Festival Fringe Firsts behind him – including the enormously successful *Linnaeus* in the city's Botanic Gardens.

Wednesday night sees them all burning the midnight oil right through to 4 a.m. in the city centre attic flat of Goran Simić. Simić has written the libretto following a visit over Christmas by Osborne. They decided to stage the opera on the

51

night of December 20 over a bottle of brandy with Spahic: the gestation period of this piece is truncated to put it mildly. "A new opera would normally take me two years," Osborne observes disarmingly. "I suppose this has taken six weeks in all... ".

Osborne is alternately composing at the piano and scribbling musical notation. His assistant and collaborator, Bennett Hogg, is working on the orchestra scores, and Scottish music journalist Susan Nickalls is busy with pencil and Tippex pasting up and copying the scores. Toby and Rocky move around the floor to the children's parts.

Goran is entertaining at the other end of the steeply-eaved open plan living area. The Austrian ambassador is assisting him in the demolition of a bottle of brandy, together with a group of Italian aid workers who regularly travel into Sarajevo personally delivering medical supplies. "I've made sixty trips into Sarajevo in the last year," observes Luigi. Today he's brought in two rucksacks of colostomy bags.

Into this extraordinary cosmopolitan mayhem pops the energetic figure of the British ambassador, Robert Barnett. He seems young for an ambassador – he's forty actually – amazingly enthusiastic and he's a real brick. He's helped out with food, transport, notebooks and pencils – and now he carries off the newly crafted scores for photocopying at the embassy. He's the sort of chap who makes you feel proud to carry a British passport.

It is in this pulsating environment, redolent of student days in freezing garrets, that composition of the opera is completed at 2 a.m. on Saturday morning, just four days before the Tuesday night opening. Osborne is frank. "There's quite a lot of Wagner, Beethoven, Debussy and Mendelssohn, I'm afraid. But, after all, this piece is a Museum of Europe. It's a matter of time and careful theft, as well." Each of the remaining high pressure days will bring its own series of logistical problems peculiar to working with an *ad hoc* team in a city under almost complete siege.

Just finding enough bread to make sandwiches for 120 rehearsing children is a daunting task which Rocky and Toby take on at the crack of dawn each morning, scouring the city for bakers who will sell them bread. Finding bottles of Coca Cola for thirsty children is even more difficult.

The smoke machine which was supposed to be smuggled into the city has not turned up. There is no gas oil for the theatre's emergency generators. This has to be found from somewhere for the actual performance as the electricity supply is liable to interruption. The production budget is being exceeded. That having been said, it is quite ludicrously low for a production involving use of a national theatre, 46-piece Symphony Orchestra, choir of 120 children, 20 or so singers, and all the technical and design paraphernalia. With a budget of just 10,000 Deutschmarks, Osborne is certainly equalling his record for speed with that of consummate financial skill. Three thousand Deutschmarks will come from cash raised in Edinburgh. Osborne, who is daily looking more like an angel in every sense of the word, has guaranteed orchestra and performers payment from his own pocket.

Bennett Hogg is helping Osborne with the conducting of the orchestra. He teaches part-time composition at the City University in London and at Norwich Art School. He is not so laid back as Osborne. He is increasingly concerned about the string section of the orchestra. On Monday, he admits, "This is truly crisis day." The orchestra have but two days effectively to rehearse and learn the entire operetta. Many of the hurriedly-copied scores have wrong notes and in photocopying passages at the bottoms of pages have disappeared. The physical condition of the strings is poor and there are only half the number of string players there should be: many have been killed and others have simply slipped away from Sarajevo. As first violin Gordana rather succinctly puts it, "We are an orchestra of survivors." But the patience of the orchestra is also under pressure. "There's a fine balance today between them just losing their temper and walking out," worries Bennett.

By the end of the day, however, things are coming together. Hogg is more cheerful, triumphant even. "I would say they're playing with more spirit than the Royal Opera House Orchestra."

Composer Nigel Osborne with the personable and charming Foreign Minister of Bosnia Herzogovena, Irfan Ljubijankić, at the opera *Europe*. Irfan Ljubijankić died on May 28, 1995 when his helicopter was shot down by Croatian Serb forces over the Bihać enclave. *February 1995*

Sarajevo winter, 1993. After almost two years of siege, the Bosnian capital is a mass of tangled wreckage and shattered buildings. Children play with snowballs in front of one of the two shattered Unis Towers, destroyed in May 1992 by Serb anti-aircraft fire used ground-to-ground. Beyond is the square bulk of the Holiday Inn Hotel, then home to most of the city's press corps and once virtually immune to all the ordinance which rained all around. In this photograph, members of the French anti-sniper squad are taking up position to cover an evacuation of the sick and elderly. *December 1993*

If Bennett thought Monday was bad, Tuesday develops into a living nightmare. As Osborne puts it to the cast. "We have rehearsals at three and five in the afternoon – then the main rehearsal at eight."

Of course, as everyone knows, it has to be all right on the night. The mid-afternoon rehearsal is a disaster; a shambles. Miss Europe's microphone goes down. Then the stowaway's, the male lead. Within a few minutes one working mike is being passed from hand to hand. In the auditorium virtually no sound can be heard. Just a sort of ambient wail of distortion. Everybody stares accusingly at Bosnian TV who are to broadcast the operetta live and who are busy setting up their gear. Miss Europe is now almost in tears. Singers are shrugging their shoulders. They look ready to walk off the job. Only the children carry on singing angelically without any need for amplification.

The problem is simple. The answer is not. The batteries on all the mikes – unused for so long – are exhausted. And there is no source in Sarajevo for the small 'Triple A' batteries. This is the opportunity for the BBC to come to the rescue. Reporter Jim Muir heads back to their base at the city's Holiday Inn and returns with batteries to save the day.

The five o'clock rehearsal is a major improvement. But the performance at eight in the richly gilded theatre before 1,000 people is a moving, emotional *tour de force* which sees orchestra, singers and children in almost perfect harmony. Prime

53

Minister Haris Silajdić, Foreign Minister Irfan Ljubijankić and half of the government gather in the official box and smile down with evident satisfaction on the story of the not so good ship 'Europe' aboard which a stowaway has been found. Replies the stowaway, "On this ship I have always been, I bought my ticket 1,000 years ago." And Miss Europe admits, "I lost the maps – that's the truth." And the children sing plaintively,

> *Do the birds have a nationality,*
> *Does the wind belong to someone,*
> *Does the rain change its name,*
> *When it falls on some river,*
> *Maybe our ancestors know,*
> *Oh Europe, you please tell us.*

The audience of Sarajijle cannot be said to receive this ecstatically. You get the impression they are, quite simply, bemused. Bemused by the temporary return of such richness and beauty to their city.

Despite the most extreme of privations – lack of food, water, electricity and gas – an extraordinary feature of the siege of Sarajevo has been the conscious maintenance of human dignity. One feature of this has been the defiant way in which the women of Sarjevo have dressed so elegantly to go out on the streets of their shattered capital. This lady has donned her best furs to venture out to the market. *February 1995*

55

Top: German operated C-160 Transall transport aircraft lands at Sarajevo airport. From the summer of 1992 through to spring 1995 the capital and its population of almost 400,000 people was sustained by the UNHCR airlift into the capital. The airlift was always operated according to the whims of the besieging Serb gunners and was frequently interrupted. In spring 1995 the Serbs refused to further guarantee the safety of the airlift leading to near starvation for the civilian population. *March 1993*

Above: Although, from time to time, during the siege of Sarajevo goods appeared plentiful in the market they were, in fact, generally smuggled, highly restricted in quantity and far outwith the pockets of most of the population. *February 1995*

Cellist Vedran Smailović, often called 'The Soul of Sarajevo', plays in the ruins of the concert hall of the Skenderija Stadium together with composer Nigel Osborne from Edinburgh. *March 1993*

The opera *Europe,* written and produced by Edinburgh music professor Nigel Osborne, was the first dramatic performance to take place in Sarajevo's National Theatre since the outbreak of war. *February 1995*

In the freezing cold rehearsal room of Sarajevo's National Theatre, a photograph of Tito still dominates proceedings. Here two of the actors playing in the opera *Europe* rehearse their roles. *February 1995*

Sarajevo's last bookshop. Owner Elvedin professed that business was still good. "People are reading plenty. What else is there to do around here?" Even on the coldest of winter days, he carried stock out of his shop and piled it on a trestle table in the street. His shop was only 100 yards from the site of the infamous bread queue massacre of May 1992.

Nearly all the books were, of course, second-hand and relatively highly priced – in the ubiquitous Deutschmark. Virtually no books could be produced any longer in a city without paper and where printing machines lay smashed or idle. At the front of Elvedin's stall there lay, poignantly, a Serbo-Croat edition of Mario Vargas Llosa's *The War at the End of the World. February 1994*

The constant search for water involved even the youngest who often carried their contribution ten, twelve or fifteen storeys up shattered apartment blocks. These children have collected their water in empty European Union cooking oil containers. *December 1993*

Sarajevo's Lion Cemetery. The cemeteries gradually encroached on every piece of parkland, football pitch or any other green space in the city. Beyond the cemetery is the Zetra Stadium where Torvill and Dean skated their way to Gold Medal victory in the Sarajevo Winter Olympics. *December 1993*

64 Bosnian government fighter defends the suburb of Hrašno. Just one hundred metres away are the Serb positions in Grbavica. *February 1994*

Cradle of War

The Northern Corridor

"Take us to kill Croatian *ustaše* in Brčko!" Camouflage-clad young Rade gestures insistently with his Kalashnikov and breathes his beery breath on us through a set of spectacularly broken teeth. Waylaid outside a smoke-filled bar packed with soldiers in Prnjavor in northern Bosnia, we could hardly fail to be impressed by his zeal for killing Croatian 'fascists'. But it was against our better judgement that my driver Igor and I reluctantly agreed to take him and his fellow fighter, Goran, to the front. We were in the so-called 300 kilometre long 'northern corridor' and only too well aware that to have two uniformed and armed Serbs with us could indeed be something of a mixed blessing: on the one hand, a distinct advantage at the Serb checkpoints for two journalists travelling on dubious accreditation in a sensitive zone but, on the other hand, a tempting target for the Croatian snipers and mortar positions just two or three kilometres to the north and south of the road.

The 'northern corridor' snakes its tortuous way through northern and eastern Bosnia, connecting Serbia proper to the Serb strongholds in Bosnia and Krajina. It is the only supply link: as such it is not only the indispensable key to the creation of a Greater Serbia, but it has also set the seal of doom on the Vance-Owen agreement, which grants control to Bosnian Croats of one salient cutting through the link, and another finger of land is awarded to the Muslims. Bosnian Serb leader Radovan Karadžić has declared continued control of the road as, quite simply, "a matter of life and death" for Bosnia's Serbs and, accordingly, could not recommend to the so-called Bosnian Serb Parliament meeting in Bijeljina, on April 25 1993, acceptance of the Vance-Owen peace plan.

Until August 1992, parts of the northern corridor were held by Croat and Muslim forces making the passage of Serb supplies and war materials virtually impossible. So, that summer, Serb forces drove a 10 kilometre wide corridor through their enemies' positions. Although this strategic corridor was heavily defended, it has always remained under constant pressure.

The evidence of this was to be seen on both sides of the improvised route. Not just in the shattered buildings or, indeed, the shell and mortar holes in the road itself, but in the Bosnian Serb military presence: aged T55 and T72 tanks, a few of the more sophisticated M84s; military trucks and buses packed with soldiers continually on the move; and tense groups of soldiers or white-belted military police in control of every junction and crossroads. Now a tarmacadamed road, then little more than a cart track, now a newly-built stretch of wide dirt track, we alternately sped and lurched past towns now bloody legends in this, the toughest of conflicts. We drive through the rolling countryside and fertile soil of the Sava valley to Derventa – the deserted apartment blocks on its northern outskirts presenting their blackened, shell-shattered facades to a wasteland of destruction, the smaller dwellings once standing in their shadow now reduced to piles of rubble.

Then, along the banks of the River Bosna to Modriča – early last summer riven by war. When I stood above the city the previous May, I observed its gradual destruction as both sides poured shells into the other's sector. Now I could observe the incontrovertible evidence of its pointless destruction. As we rumbled over an improvised Bailley-type bridge, I passed under the hill where I stood less than a year ago and witnessed those early throes of death.

And on to Brčko where, a year previously, I had watched maybe 15,000 people flee in one single weekend. Now the ruins of a once thriving industrial city and port on the Sava were eerily deserted. The northern and eastern suburbs of the city were still being fought over. Brčko was one of the few parts of Bosnia where the Muslim-Croat military alliance still survived against a common Serb enemy, whilst Muslim and Croat fought it out in central Bosnia.

Meantime, from the back seat, we are treated to a relentless diatribe from young Rade. Three years in the army and he has absorbed some curious ideas. He is convinced that Germany and the US will attack the Serbs of former Yugoslavia. "We are ready for them. We will destroy them." Now an afterthought. "Will you English also attack us?" I neatly side-step this one in my usual way. "I am from Scotland. You should understand Scotland is a separate nation from England. We are different." He seems to be well satisfied by this explanation.

Now comes a mildly sensational piece of news to which we have not been privy. "Already we have shot down one US AWACS plane." This is announced with evident pride as his finger insistently jabs my shoulder. "Be sure you write this truth in your newspaper." His friend, Goran, unnervingly prepares his Kalashnikov for firing. I am not altogether sure whether this relates to the prevailing tension within the car or to the roadside dangers. Weapons handling is not a strong point with these chaps. They tend to treat their guns like movie props. NATO no-fly-zone or not, two Gazelle helicopters fly low overhead barely above tree-height in the direction of military headquarters in Banja Luka.

As we reach the checkpoint at Modriča, the bombastic Rade has a change of mind. He is not going to kill *ustaše* in Brčko after all. We are glad of this, if only to rid ourselves of our increasingly tiresome passenger. Instead, he now plans to meet up with military drinking buddies in Modriča Lug. We are mightily relieved as he lurches off and I am gratified to note that he is stopped by the military police and appears to be getting a hard time about the state of his travel papers.

Near to Brčko, Goran leaves us for his unit and we are now on our own to deal with the military checkpoints. It is mid-afternoon and our progress comes to a halt at the checkpoint outside the eastern Bosnian town of Bijeljina. Passports and press cards are this time insufficient to get us through a rather more thorough check. We lack the necessary permission from military headquarters in Banja Luka. Of this I am well aware. I also know we would never have been granted permission to travel this road so I hadn't bothered rolling up in Banja Luka to be kept waiting in order to learn this rather obvious piece of information.

We are detained at the side of the road by a not unfriendly group of military police and their less compromising commander. They are all fascinated by my British-registered Skoda motor car. Part wonderment at how it managed to get to the war zones of former Yugoslavia, part amazement that a western journalist apparently can't afford more opulent transport. The hours pass and darkness falls. Around 8 p.m. we are instructed to proceed to the nearest police station and from there are taken to the local HQ of the Office of National Security where our passports are confiscated. We are lodged overnight in the local hotel. Or at least that is what it was in better times. It is now a hostel for soldiers and shows signs of military abuse: the wardrobe in my room appears to have been opened with a Kalashnikov. Bullet holes are splayed across both doors, both of which now flap uselessly open.

Questioning starts at 8 a.m. prompt. It is something of a parody of interrogation techniques; second rate B-movie stuff. A plainclothes officer does it from the textbook. "It is no use to deny things. We know that your passports are forgeries. You must confess what you are doing here." Igor gets the treatment first.

Waiting in the corridor outside I am earnestly engaged in conversation in halting German by a burly bull-headed, but altogether genial, denizen of Serbian Security. He tells me he must learn German for his job. He clutches a thick, well-thumbed dictionary in his hand. I ask him in a simple sentence if Bijeljina is his home town. He refers to the dictionary looking up the word town, the word home, and so on. Communication is slow and ponderous. His job is apparently very important.

"When the Germans come and attack us it will be my job to interrogate the prisoners." This could be a long war. Meantime, he is conscientiously taking every opportunity to spruce up his command of the language. Our conversation comes to an end as I am summoned for interview by a gap-toothed, leather-jacketed operative of state security.

My questioners have a basic problem. As they do not speak English – and I am not prepared to admit to any knowledge of Serbian – they are obliged to use Igor for translation. The interview accordingly is leisurely in its progress and working out acceptable answers is not that difficult.

Igor: " These chaps say your passport is forged. That's not true is it?" "Now they say you're a spy. That's nonsense isn't it?" Establishment of my own identity beyond the shadow of a doubt is not too difficult either: press cards from the UN, Republic of Krajina and Tanjug in Belgrade; letters from the editor of *Scotland on Sunday* and the BBC; driving licence, credit cards, National Library of Scotland reading room ticket and Amnesty International card – this last seemingly impressing them the most. I shower them with pieces of paper, all of which are religiously photocopied.

My questioner is fast building up a thick file. This is clearly Very Important. I am asked how many times I have visited the war zones of Yugoslavia.

When I reply "twenty-eight" my questioner starts to look mildly shell-shocked. Instead of holding back, I bombard him with quite useless and irrelevant bits of information: a description of the long journey by car from Scotland, my work and holidays in Yugoslavia before the war, and so on, and so on.

Eventually, he barks out a command to a colleague outside the door. Nothing as final or exciting as instructions to form up a firing squad. The door opens and a tray laden with glasses, coffee and real Napoleon brandy (stolen from an impounded lorry parked outside) appear as if by magic. Now, the business apparently over, all is, quite suddenly, smiles and bonhomie. We are obliged to remain another hour to drain the bottle with our erstwhile captors after which, amidst much back slapping and handshaking, we are waved merrily on our way. Control over drinking and driving is clearly not a priority around here.

Beyond Bijeljina, the northern corridor ends at the Serbian border at Pavlovica Most, the newly constructed bridge over the Drina, privately financed by a Chicago-based millionaire originally from Serbia, Slobodan Pavlović, in order to link Serb communities in eastern Bosnia with their brothers over the river in Serbia. From here it is but an hour's drive into the centre of Belgrade.

In the increasingly beleaguered and shabby capital the view from the ground is much the same as in northern Bosnia. At an exhibition of photographs in The Museum of Applied Arts, which graphically illustrates the horrors of the war albeit in a partisan manner, an intelligent and clearly cultured lady asks, "Why is the whole world against the Serbs? Will the Americans bomb us? You know this all just a continuation of the Second World War.

Muslims, Croatians and the Germans want to make the Fourth Reich here."

She is typical of an uncomprehending, increasingly embittered and once moderate middle class. Fed on a diet of propaganda purveyed by state controlled TV and Milosevic's newspaper *Politika*, these poor people believe, at best, that the West has turned its back on all Serbs and, at worst, that a vast international conspiracy seeks to crush them.

In parallel with this disappointment, the extremists flourish in Belgrade. Private armies and local warlords recruit openly. The black marketeers and organised criminals grow fat: the new BMWs, Mercedes and Intercoolers crowd the streets outside the more expensive and fashionable bars and restaurants. And for the privileged few strolling on the fashionable Terazija, there are Yves Rocher cosmetics from France, La Perla lingerie from Italy, Hugo Boss shirts and socks from Germany, the newest Panasonic faxes from Japan and the latest Levi 501s.

Nationalist geegaws are sold on the streets by wild-eyed bearded men leaping to the strains of patriotic music. And all the while, in a capital suffering fifty per cent unemployment and an inflation rate of five per cent a day, the poor shuffle their miserable shabby way past these proponents of the glories of a Greater Serbia.

At the exhibition of *Genocide Against the Serbs*, there is a photograph of Croatian President Franjo Tudjman meeting with Pope John Paul. The caption explains that this is evidence of the coordinated advance of German and Croatian fascism from the north and the expansionism of the Vatican from the east.

Whether in Srpska, Krajina, or Serbia itself, the prevailing mood amongst Serbs was unmistakable. It was of a society consumed by paranoia, utterly convinced of a world conspiracy against a cruelly misunderstood and noble people unjustly denied their place at the table of great nations.

Woman in bus queue, Belgrade *September 1993*

Right: Three months into war in Bosnia and there was a brief flicker of hope for opposition parties in Belgrade who banded together under the banner of DEPOS. In spite of support from disparate opposition groups of royalists, clergy, Chetniks and students, the demonstrations, organised in protest against the Milosević regime, fizzled out after three days or so, despite the arrival of Crown Prince Alexander from London. Refugees still slept in the streets and the government carried on printing money. If anything, Milosević emerged stronger from the threat to his leadership ... and Alexander returned to London. In actual fact, many of the 'opposition' groups were distinctly unprepossessing and more nationalist than even Milosević. *June 1992*

Left: More than 2,000 students at Belgrade University occupied the city centre campus in protest against Milosević and the prosecution of war in Bosnia. A spokesman for the President alleged on television that the students were each paid 100 deutschmarks for every night they 'sat in' at the university. These payments were allegedly made by foreign intelligence services. Students then photocopied more than 100,000 DM 100 notes and 'paid' themselves. The photocopied notes became the official currency on the besieged campus. In the photograph, Ivana is cutting up the copied currency while student leader Goran checks their finished quality. *June 1992*

Above: Nun with latest model video camera at DEPOS demonstrations. *June 1992*

Serbian nationalist
supporters of Crown
Prince Alexander.
June 1992

72

74

Left: Sanctions and shopping. Even under the worst of sanctions, for those with money every imaginable commodity was always available in the Serbian capital of Belgrade. An exclusive Belgrade patisserie opened in 1993 at the height of sanctions. Twix bars, Wrigleys Spearmint Gum and home cooked delicacies crowd the shelves. A single cake cost the equivalent of two months old age pension but the shop assistant told me, "We are sold out every day. There are plenty of people with a lot of money in Belgrade." *April 1993*

Below: Marija owned a small village shop near the town of Usče in central Serbia. When I visited her, inflation was running at one and a half billion per cent, she could only get some prepackaged supplies, marked up her prices up by up to 200% a day and had to pay off the financial police when they come to call. In Usče, a deputation had just been to see the chief of police to tell him that the townspeople were faced with the prospect of having to steal bread to live. *September 1993*

Above: Shopfront, Peć, Kosovo *August 1993*

The lush landscape of Kosovo laid out below the Albanian border. Yugoslav army soldiers patrol near Kafa Prusit *August 1993*

Yugoslav army soldier lost in thought, Albanian border. *August 1993*

Children in the market in Priština, capital of the formerly autonomous province of Kosovo. Milosević has revoked the autonomous status granted by Tito. More than 90% of the population in this province of Serbia is ethnically Albanian. *August 1993*

An ethnic Albanian peasant takes his new freezer
home by horse and cart, Kosovo Polje.
August 1993

The Bosnian Serb press and information office in Belgrade. Despite the courtesy and normalcy of the Republika Srpska staff working there, the array of posters on the wall proclaiming the imagined dangers of German fascism and Muslim fundamentalism evidenced a quite extraordinary paranoia.

September 1993

'Warring Parties'

Bringing a Tear to The Eye of a War Criminal …

Buses, cars and lorries in the frontline Serbian town of Benkovac have his photograph pasted to their windscreens. He may be universally feared and hated by Croats and Muslims, but Serbs here are ecstatic about the arrival of a man known simply as 'Arkan' in their midst.

As he emerges from his brand new, jet black Mitsubishi Intercooler Turbo – the long wheelbase, 180 horsepower model fitted with the very latest American Motorola communications equipment – there can be no denying the all pervasive charisma of the man. Clean shaven, immaculately turned out in his newly pressed camouflage uniform, the dark blue beret worn pizza-style, and the deeply tanned good looks all combine to present a vastly different impression from that of the usual scruffy, dissolute soldiery in this war. When he eases off the Ray-Ban glasses, it is then that you can discern the menace in the ice-cool gaze. Supremely confident and, alternately, charming and sarcastic to those around him, I was soon aware that I was are in the sinister presence of a psychopath. Imprisoned in peace time in half a dozen countries in Europe, hunted by Interpol and named as a war criminal for his now legendary brutality and that of his elite forces, you are in the presence of a man not to be meddled with. Nor his retainers, the so-called Serbian Tigers (Arkan keeps a full grown tiger as a pet), the Serbian Volunteer Guard, or Arkanovci as they are often known.

Just over a week previously, they were alerted from their base in the Kosovo region of Serbia by the Croatian breakthrough into the Serbian Republic of Krajina. Two days later, Arkan and his men rolled up in the frontline town of Benkovac: the officers in their Mitsubishi Intercoolers, the soldiers in their modern Austrian-manufactured Pinzgauer all-terrain trucks, manufactured in Austria by Steyer Daimler Puch. Within hours they had taken control of the town with checkpoints on all roads in and out; their headquarters were established in the hotel, after summary ejection of the residents, including a group of grateful French UN soldiers being held by the local Krajina forces; and defensive trenches and positions were soon being prepared. Within 48 hours, the Tigers were down at the frontline attacking and teasing the Croatians at the most threatening points of their advance. Near to the twisted wreckage of the Maslenica Bridge, a small group operating by night penetrated the Croatian defences around the town of Novigrad and wreaked havoc before slipping away into the darkness without casualty. The next day they successfully re-took two villages from the Croats. The incentives for operational efficiency are considerable: any of Arkan's men wounded or killed in action receives a solid gold medal. Equally, any man in danger of capture is required to pull the pin on a grenade and self-destruct. Failure to observe this code of honour results in certain expulsion, if not death, at the hands of erstwhile colleagues.

You might expect the leader of such a feared and extraordinarily efficient unit to have an impeccable military background. He is brash and self-effacing when he talks of his career to date. In fact, Arkan, real name Zeljko Raznjatović, was born forty years ago and trained as an apprentice confectioner. Whilst his broadly legal activities these days embrace ice cream parlours in Belgrade and Presidency of the Red Star football team, his extensive illegal activities stretch back to when he was 14 and was imprisoned in Belgrade for housebreaking.

Varied talents subsequently manifested themselves. First of all, there was a series of offences in Zagreb which brought a three year sentence there in 1969; he was leader of a prison revolt in Milan in 1973, followed by flight to Frankfurt where the theft of jewellery provided him with travel funds; five bank raids in Gothenburg (1975); a series of crimes in Holland, Belgium and England culminating in his arrest whilst committing a bank robbery in Brussels, following which he served two months of a ten year sentence before a dramatic escape in which he broke both legs. A trail of criminal chaos followed him through Oslo, Copenhagen, Brussels (again), Frankfurt, Milan (again), Athens and back to Belgrade. A fervent anti-communist, he was re-arrested in Zagreb in November 1990 in possession

War criminal and paramilitary leader Zeljko Raznjatović, known as 'Arkan'. *February 1993*

of illegal weapons; he was now building up his force of Tigers against the coming breakdown of the Communist system in Yugoslavia.

His men are highly disciplined and well trained. Their checkpoint techniques around Benkovac could only be compared in these war zones to those of the French paras. While your papers are thoroughly checked, two other soldiers have moved close in to the car with a clear view of all passengers, their fingers already on the triggers of their apparently new and scrupulously maintained machine guns. Another soldier covers from a distance. There is nothing casual about these men who rise every morning at 6 a.m. for sport, exercises, and lessons in strategy and tactics. Then there is a parade in full uniform. "The world should know that we are not brigands with long hair, beards and knives between our teeth," says Arkan. In the afternoon, there is instruction in hand to hand fighting, house to house fighting, obstacle courses and weapons training. All men are fully trained in care and maintenance of their weapons: soldiers have light machine guns, Kalashnikov variations and FN rifles. The officers field the neat snub-nosed Scorpios and Ingrams; Arkan prefers his Heckler & Koch which is always at his side in operational situations.

All his men regard Arkan as a father figure. The fierce discipline is leavened by his help for any man with personal problems. If you wish to join up with the Tigers then there is a daily recruiting session at Arkan's Belgrade *Ari* coffee house. He does not deny that many of those showing up are either criminals or refugees from bodies like the French Foreign Legion.

By the time full scale war broke out in Croatia in the summer of 1991, Arkan was out of his prison cell in Zagreb and ready for action. He and his force of almost 1,000 men moved into the eastern Slavonia region in support of local insurrectionist Serbs. In his own words to me: "I will go anywhere in defence of Serbs. I am a Serb and the rights of Serbs, wherever they are, are my first concern." Where the fighting was fiercest, Arkan and his men were there, deploying rapidly and ruthlessly and, reportedly, in the vanguard of ethnic cleansing operations. When the Yugoslav army attack on Vukovar ground to a halt, according to popular legend, Arkan and his men commandeered a handful of tanks and moved on the city centre. It fell within three days. His Intercoolers to this day bear Vukovar registrations in commemoration of that hour of glory: the Vukovar registrations are also notorious for their use on top class stolen vehicles. Arkan took over control of all vehicle registration in the ruined city. Later the same month, in the nearby Croatian town of Osijek, he kidnapped four nuns and demanded the corpses of four of his men in exchange. He got them.

In March 1992, the Arkanovci transferred their attentions to then largely peaceful northern areas of Bosnia. His men moved into the towns of Zvornik and Bijeljina, from where the world was treated to unedifying images of his men kicking the dead bodies of Muslim women they had just murdered. The pictures went around the world, appearing in *Newsweek*, *Time* and dozens of other newspapers and journals. It is said Arkan's rage knew no bounds and he issued a death sentence on American Ron Haviv, the photographer concerned. His paranoia was intensified when the official Bosnian news agency reported how his men nailed a Muslim Imam to the wall of his mosque whilst he was still alive.

His hatred of journalists is renowned. I was blissfully unaware of this. When he emerged from his hotel HQ in Benkovac, the Serbian press was arrayed outside. Not a camera shutter clicked and the journalist with whom I was travelling, from the Belgrade paper *Borba*, gaped in awe. It was left to yours truly to address him in an appalling mixture of Russian and Serbian. "Izvenite, mogu slikka?" (Excuse me, is it possible to take some photographs?). Of course, neither did I realise that he speaks word perfect English (and six other languages). The reply in Serbian raises a sycophantic titter amongst the Serbian journos. "Of course, it is *possible* to take photographs of me. But you have missed your chance." And he disappears in flash of polished boots and smartly pressed uniform through the door of the hotel. A bully and a smartass. But you have to admire his style nevertheless.

My colleague Dragan from *Borba* was of course

aware of the rumpus which occurred in his own newspaper office when an article critical of Arkan appeared in the newspaper. Arkan and his henchmen stormed their way in. In a misguided attempt to tame the beast the editor asked the teetotal, nonsmoking thug what he wished to drink. The response was uncompromising. "I want to drink the blood of the fucking journalists who write about me in your newspaper."

The war crimes charges levelled initially against him in the United States accused Arkan and his Tigers of the murder of some 2,000 civilians in the Zvornik-Bijeljina region. Hardly surprisingly, he does not wish to speak about the war crimes allegations. Asked in Benkovac what he felt about being wanted for war crimes he coolly observed, "I don't care a shit about what outsiders want or say. I only care for Serbs, for my people." A man with a clear, uncomplicated view.

Asked specifically about the US Secretary of State Lawrence Eagleburger's denunciation of his activities, he replies quick as a flash, "Eagleburger is the last American communist. Why should I care about the views of an extinct species?" This is the man who drinks milk shakes, abjures alcohol and smoking in his presence is forbidden. He takes pride in his status as a family man with four children: this would not, however, prevent him from taking a second wife two years later in the form of a stunningly beautiful Serbian model and pop singer. He also purports to be deeply religious. Indeed, priests visit his men on the front lines to bless their bullets.

When I speak to Arkan outside the hotel at Benkovac, a delegation of local women arrive to express their thanks to the man who is so evidently their hero. A senior, middle-aged officer in the Krajina army begs a sneering young Arkanovci of maybe twenty summers to ask his leader to come out. The bear is eventually tempted from his lair to accept gifts of cooked hams, locally-made bread, a scarf, a tapestry and a bottle of whisky. This last item is refused by the clean living warlord and he accepts the others "to give to refugees". As the women genuflect and embrace their hero a tear is brought to his eye. This is deeply moving stuff. It is also clearly the display of a highly political animal.

Politics has indeed become Arkan's latest calling. He has been since the end of 1992 a member of parliament: deputy for Kosovo where a minority of less than ten per cent of Serbs rule the majority Albanian province. The Albanians are disenfranchised, as well as without social services or education. This seems to suit Arkan. Asked how he squares his status as a deputy with his ruthless military activities he simply states, "I am a Serbian volunteer first. A Serbian nationalist. I am available wherever Serbs need help. I help in Kosovo, I help here in Benkovac." That clear view again. His benefactors gaze on in glassy-eyed adulation, clapping their hands delightedly. In Arkan's world anything and everything is justified in the cause of Serbian nationalism. Every question and accusation put to him seems to elicit the simplistic response, "I am a Serb."

Ethnic cleansing. Houses burn in northern Bosnia. *May 1992*

83

Above: Off to war with a guitar. Members of the Bosnian army 7th Korpus, Bugojno. *November 1994*

Opposite: Trench defenders of Maglaj, Bosnian army 3rd Korpus. *August 1994*

Bosnian army soldier goes off to war on a motor-bike in the hills
above Modriča. *May 1992*

Don Quixote. Bosnian army soldier rides off to war from Vitez.
May 1995

Bosnian territorial soldiers pressed into service in the north of the country celebrate. Behind this apparently joyous image lies something rather more sinister. Three Catholic soldiers display a trophy of war: an Orthodox cross taken that morning from a Serb they have killed.
April 1992

88

Top left: Lost in thought. Croatian territorials stare across the river into Bosnia, near to Bosanska Dubica. *September 1991*

Bottom left: Young Serbian soldiers on a tank training course at Manjača, near to Banja Luka. *May 1993*

Above: Croatian soldier makes his way ashore from a military ferry over the River Sava. He has been fighting in the Orasje salient in northern Bosnia. At the time, the presence of the Croatian army in Bosnia was regarded as secret. *August 1993*

Above: Serb extremist, or Chetnik, soldier outside the Cafe Borik, Turbe, on the frontline with Bosnian government forces. *December 1992*

Right: Croatian extremist soldiers of the HVO travel up the route carved out by the British Royal Engineers over Vran Mountain between Tomislavgrad and Prozor. Known as Route Triangle to UN forces and journalists, this was formerly a logging track expanded into a road suitable for convoys and other traffic. The day that this picture was taken the road had been closed by the Royal Engineers for repair and they had parked their Saxon armoured personnel carrier across the route. This was rather ungraciously accepted by the boys of the HVO and weapons were loaded by the Brits when the swastika-sporting locals tried to push their way through. *April 1994*

Left: Men of The Royal Highland Fusiliers on checkpoint duty, Stari Vitez, Christmas Day. *December 1994*

Above: Warrior armoured fighting vehicle crew of Battle Group Alpha (1st Battalion Devon & Dorset Regiment) loaded up and ready to go at Vitez base. *May 1995*

In September 1994 a top level delegation of US Generals secretly visited Bosnia on a mission to assess the situation should sanctions be lifted by the US and in a bid to support the Muslim-Croat confederation cemented in Washington the previous March.

Above: 4-star USAF General 'Chuck' Boyd visits the memorial to the first British soldier to die in Bosnia, Corporal Wayne Edwards of the Welch Fusiliers. *Second from left* Brigadier General Hayden (USAF), Head of Intelligence US European Command and, next to him, in dark glasses, is the US Ambassador in Sarajevo, Victor Jakovec. *Extreme right* Brigadier Andrew Ridgway, UN commander Sector South West.

Right: General Boyd talks with 7th Korpus Bosnian General Filip Alagić in Gornji Vakuf.

Rebuilding Bridges

"I really love this city," declares Jimmy Kennedy, field director of the charity *War Child* in East Mostar. You do not doubt his sincerity but just *why* may not immediately be so apparent. Mostar – once the architectural and cultural jewel of Bosnia Herzegovena – is now a city of decapitated minarets, shell-shattered domes and once grand Austro-Hungarian facades, at best just pitted by large calibre bullet holes – at worst empty, windowless and roofless shells. In the whole of East Mostar there is not one single building undamaged by three years of war. Even blighted Sarajevo cannot be compared to this vista of universal destruction.

When war broke out in Bosnia in the spring of 1992, Serbian forces attacked from the hills to the east of the ancient city. The location is at once its advantage and the explanation for its fall. Mostar is dramatically situated in a great bowl of land, dominated by the sunburnt scrub and the limestone *karst* of the mountains of Herzegovena on the east and west banks of the green waters of the Neretva River. Mostar's historic importance – and, indeed, its fate today – has always been based upon its geographical position near the mouth of the Neretva valley and at the strategic junction of roads running north, south and west. Combined with its dramatic mix of cultures and Christian, Orthodox and Muslim religions, the city has oft been regarded as the true meeting point of east and west.

Although the Muslims and Croats of Mostar repulsed the Serbs in 1992, the seeds of instability were planted and many people now think that its death knell was the ill-fated Vance-Owen plan which prompted local Croats under their warlord Mate Boban to evict the Muslim population from the city, in advance of its anticipated allocation as a Croatian canton, and its establishment as the capital of the Croat statelet of Herzog Bosna. In the ensuing onslaught, the Muslim population in West Mostar – some 25,000 – was evicted and driven across the river onto the east bank. The social fabric of Mostar, its strong cultural traditions, its traditional multi-ethnic make-up – and its breathtaking *melange* of eastern and western architecture – all largely disappeared in a matter of months. One by one, the five bridges over the river linking the two communities fell.

The lasting image of this destruction came in November 1993 when tank shells fired by the Croatian Defence Force tumbled the oldest bridge into the waters of the Neretva. The Stari Most, adjudged "one of the most beautiful bridges in the world" by Rebecca West on her journey through Yugoslavia in 1937, was built 420 years ago by the architect Hajrudin under the orders of the Turkish Sultan, Süleyman the Magnificent. With its high, steeply curved single arch span, held in place by a mixture of horsehair and eggshell, its design was revolutionary: if it were to fall down, the Sultan instructed, then its builder would be executed. It did not. For four centuries it survived as a symbol of the meeting of east and west, steadfast survivor of more than twenty earthquakes and countless Balkan wars, until November 1993, that is. The physical reality of the Mostar of Rebecca West, observed in her classic *Black Lamb and Grey Falcon* was a vista "exquisitely planned, its towers refined by the influence of the minarets, its red-roofed houses lying among the plumy foliage of their walled gardens". That is now but a memory. Virtually all of its once famed cultural activity had disappeared by the time Croats and Muslims of Croatia and Bosnia signed up for a new federation in Washington in March 1994.

Then the city came under a two year EU administration, headed by German mayor Hans Koschnick. Although there is little sign of any lasting rapprochement between east and west banks of the river, such is the deep and lasting bitterness, some semblance of normal life is reappearing. Enterprising charities like *War Child* are behind much of this recovery.

War Child, the creation of British film makers Bill Leeson and David Wilson, came to Mostar to bake bread using a mobile military bakery bought from the British Ministry of Defence. As Tom Stoppard put it, "There is something direct and symbolic about going to where people are hungry and baking bread. It is a biblical idea. Everyone knows what a

97

Jimmy Kennedy, field director of War Child, Mostar.
April 1995

loaf of bread is and what a hungry child is." The film makers had been moved by the plight of Yugoslavia's victims of war whilst shooting a documentary for *Arena* and, as Wilson puts it, "The film making came to a stop. We soon found that baking bread was a full time occupation."

Jimmy Kennedy, the unpaid field director of *War Child*, is not what you might expect. The aid organisations in Bosnia tend to be headed up by the sort of earnest, plummy voiced Englishman you might expect to find in the pages of Somerset Maugham. Aside from being a long time friend and colleague of Leeson, 52-year-old Kennedy's lifetime occupation until last year was as a professional gambler – mainly horses and cards. "I was a good poker player," he reflects as if it were part of his past, then corrects himself, "I am!" He's as London as they come, left school at 15 and worked on building sites. Down at UNHCR headquarters they refer to him – affectionately – as 'Del Boy'. Like the Pied Piper of Hamelin, wherever his hunched figure moves in Mostar – he was injured at birth – he's relentlessly pursued by hordes of children who have immortalised him in graffiti 'Jimmy We Love You.' This is not just because he has baked some three million loaves of bread, but maybe something to do with the eight tons of Topic bars he wheedled out of the manufacturers for the children of Mostar.

Around the corner from his east bank flat – newly repaired and fitted out for him by the people of the city – is the shell of the 19th century Music School building. On the facing west bank is the gutted ruin of the Mostar Symphony Orchestra building, a once elegant mixture of Austro-Hungarian and Moorish forms. With the bakery up and running, Jimmy felt both he and Mostar were ready for a new challenge and one day he had the idea. *War Child* launched its

largest and most ambitious project to date: a $5 million Music Centre located within the 1908 shell of the Luka Primary School, designed by award-winning London architect Nicholas Lacey.

The project is up and running – 700 cubic tons of rubble had been removed from the building by early Spring of 1995, agreement having been reached with the local authorities. The charity's showbiz connections assured it of the support of powerful figures in the music and film industries. Film director Anthony Meyer, alas, died whilst endorsing the Music Centre at a meeting at English National Opera in London, but with patrons like Brent Hansen and MTV, Juliet Stevenson, Brian Eno and David Bowie, there was a momentum behind the campaign to raise the $5 million. When construction is completed, there will be concert space, recording studios, music therapy and tuition facilities. The situation in Mostar cannot exactly be termed stable but Jimmy is clear as to why it is important to start work now. "I'm an optimist. If we make a start now I believe others will follow. Our action is a symbol." Jimmy also believes that the only hope for the future of Mostar lies with its children, and music therapy is urgently needed for the many who are traumatised. For *War Child* this is, quite simply, an attempt to harness the healing power of music where it is most needed. UNICEF has reported that the level of trauma experienced by children in Mostar was the highest documented anywhere in former Yugoslavia: over eighty per cent felt their lives no longer had any value.

When the building phase is completed, the Music Centre will be able to assist other, smaller charities working in Mostar with limited facilities. Ingo Wietzke has taken time out from his studies at the Art University of Berlin to set up photography workshops. Seven teenagers are currently studying photographic and darkroom technique on the east bank and some fifteen on the west. *Recht auf Kindheit* (Rights for Childhood) is the brainchild of Anette Zinser and Barbara Hipp from Frankfurt. They are teaching music and performance arts to children. "We aim to give children new images to replace those of war," explains Anette. Their success was evident as 70 children performed circus acts for hundreds of their fellows in an improvised corral of white-painted aid trucks.

The future of some of Mostar's older institutions is less certain. Both buildings and instruments of Mostar's Symphony Orchestra are destroyed. Surviving members of the orchestra, like flautist Muamer Kulukčija, evicted from West Mostar in ethnic cleansing, are musicians with nowhere to play. From time to time he plays on the east bank 24 hour radio station, Radio Mostar, which is now back on the air with a 1kw. transmitter courtesy of the ODA, and CDs supplied by *War Child*. Sometimes, he plays Toussaint flute solos in the street outside the gutted Symphony Orchestra building.

Mostar's Theatre is damaged and dark, part of the building turned over for use as a cinema. A short distance away the Puppet Theatre is a mess of debris. In 1945 the Jesuits gave over their chapel set in a wonderful garden as a puppet theatre for the children: ironically, it was shelled by Catholic Croats from across the river. The EU has pledged support and it seems like $150,000 of repairs will be undertaken.

Ambassador Klaus Metscher, diplomatic advisor to the EU Administration, is wary of participating in cultural regeneration. "The problem is that culture here emphasises national identity. It's easier to talk about water and electricity than about culture. Besides which, the military situation is not good. Gatherings are always dangerous." Last December there was Mostar's only concert since the war: the EU organised a chamber orchestra to play in its own headquarters.

On the city's west bank, the Gallery of Mostar has been extensively renovated and was showing a selection of paintings and sculptures by Croat artists in its cool interior. Down on the east bank of the Neretva, Ekagm Handzić painted the beautiful

ancient bridge. There is now a single suspended steel walkway over the river. It is a construction recently completed by Spanish UN soldiers. But it is hardly an object of beauty and so he sits in the spring sun painting from memory. The Spanish bridge looks sturdy enough to be permanent and whether the ancient bridge will ever be rebuilt is anybody's guess. The government in Sarajevo says it has signed a contract with the Turkish government for its reconstruction; local Croat leaders say plans have already been finalised for its rebuilding by Croat engineers.

Nearby in the heart of the ancient quarter, the *bascarjiya*, metalworker Safet Begović beats images from copper for sale to non-existent tourists. I met Safet three years ago when the Serbs were shelling the city. We spoke in German, once the language of tourism around here. I asked why he troubled to open his shop that morning. "My father and my grandfather worked in this shop. What else would you expect me to do?" Of course, since I last saw him his shop has been completely destroyed but he has already rebuilt.

I am quite stunned to find him still here and I choose from his stock a small copper plate on which the image of the ancient bridge is beaten out in the centre. This is special, if slightly imperfect: a triangular sector has been gouged out by a piece of hot, flying shrapnel.

London launch at MTV for War Child's Mostar Music Centre project. *Left to right:* Patrons Tom Stoppard, Brent Hansen of MTV and Brian Eno. *May 1995*

99

Left: During the first year of war in Bosnia, Serb forces were driven off the East bank of the River Neretva. The Bosnian flag is raised by local fighters. *August 1992*

Top: Decapitated minarets and shell shattered domes: the East bank of the Neretva looking north from the Stari Most, Mostar's ancient bridge. *August 1992*

Bottom: Detail of damage to the Austro-Hungarian Moorish-style facade of the Hotel Neretva. *April 1995*

Above: Professor Salih Rajković used to work with the museum on Mostar's East bank. Pictured here on the metal suspension bridge which has replaced the Stari Most, the ruins of his museum can be seen directly behind him. *April 1995*

Right: The worn marble stones of the steeply curved Stari Most. This photograph was taken early in the war and the bridge has not yet sustained major damage. *August 1992*

The ancient Stari Most built some 420 years ago on the orders of Süleyman the Magnificent. Its architect, Hajrudin, was told that if the bridge – with its unusual steeply arched design – fell down, then he would be executed by order of the Turkish Sultan. Held together by a mixture of horse hair and eggshell, the bridge held up, much to the amazement of some of Hajrudin's contemporaries. That is, of course, until it was demolished by Croat tank shells in November 1993. *August 1992*

The entire structure of the ancient bridge tumbled into the River Neretva. In 1995, Spanish soldiers of the United Nations force, SPANBAT, based in Mostar, replaced the ancient bridge with a steel suspension bridge. Hardly an object of such beauty, it did, nevertheless, appear to be disturbingly permanent. Meantime, the government in Sarajevo has signed a contract with the Turkish government to rebuild the ancient bridge. The Croats say that engineers from Zagreb will rebuild the bridge ... *April 1995*

Metalworker Safet Begović has his shop on the edge of the western end of the Stari Most. Here his father and grandfather before him worked and there they have all sold the images of the bridge they fashion from copper. In spite of the devastation all around, his shop was restored and open again within a couple of months of the cessation of fighting. *April 1995*

Left: Muamer Kulukčija is the flautist with nowhere to play. He used to play in the Mostar Symphony Orchestra which no longer exists. When fighting broke out between Croats and Muslims in Mostar he was driven from his home on the West bank. The magnificent building of the symphony orchestra was destroyed in the fighting and here he plays outside the ruins. *April 1995*

Above and right: The notice outside the 16th century Karadjozbegova mosque on the East bank recalls better days. It says, in six languages, *You Can Visit this Mosque.* Of course, there are no longer any tourists. And there are shell holes in its ancient fabric. *April 1995*

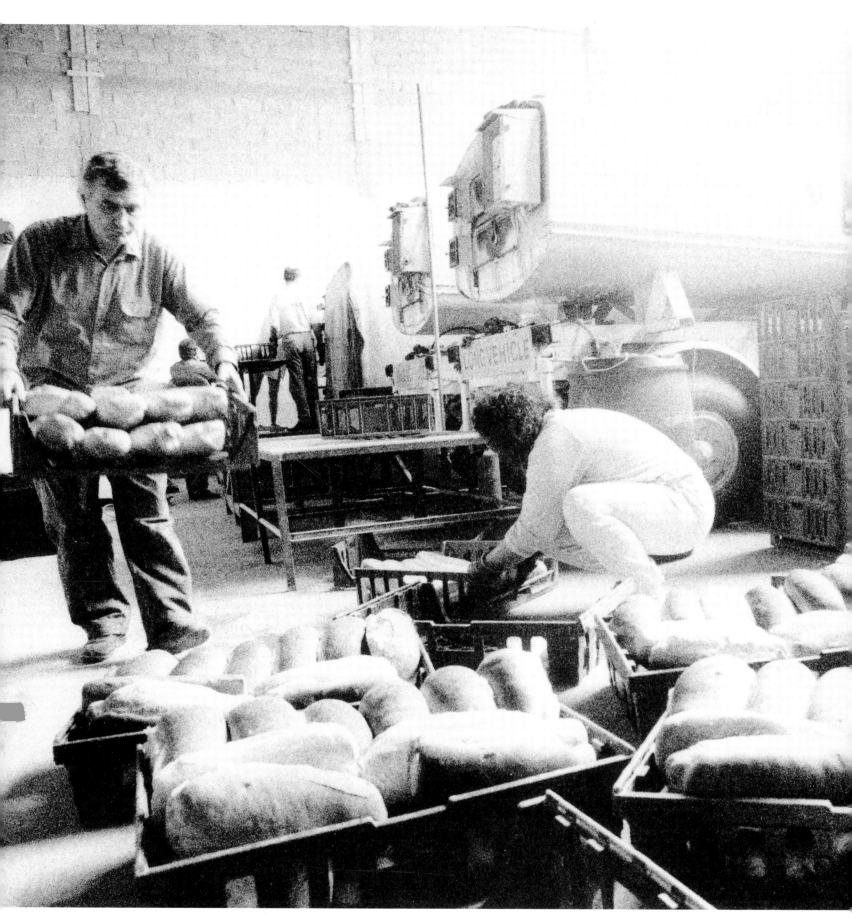

The charity War Child brought a mobile bakery to Mostar in the wake of the Washington agreement which brought an uneasy peace to the city. The bakery, formerly used by the British army and supplied by the Overseas Development Agency, baked desperately needed bread for the inhabitants of the East bank: before the war they were supplied by the main city bakery on the West but supplies did not resume with 'peace'. *April 1995*

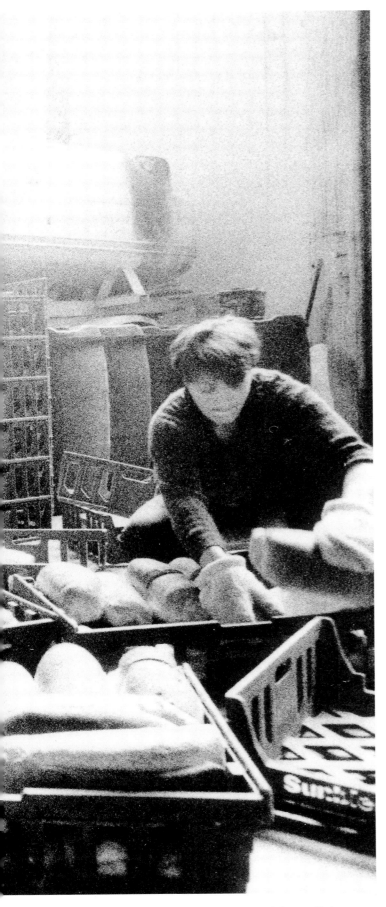

Top: Water bowser at the bakery with graffiti dedicated to field director Jimmy Kennedy.

Right: Like children anywhere those in Mostar like to dress up, paint their faces – and try to forget the grim reality of daily life. Two children dressed up for a circus organised by German aid workers. *April 1995*

The shell-shattered Austro-Hungarian facade of the Luka Primary School on Mostar's East bank. It is for this building that the charity War Child plans a $5 million music centre with performance spaces, workshop areas and facilities for music therapy. The project was unveiled at the MTV studios in London in May 1995 and it is hoped the project will be up and running by the summer of 1997. *April 1995*

When fighting broke out between Croats and Muslims in Mostar, Muslims
living on the West bank of the River Neretva were driven over to the East. The
East bank, containing most of the ancient monuments with which Mostar is so
indelibly associated, was then pounded remorselessly by Croat artillery and
hardly a single building was left undamaged. Nevertheless, people doggedly
continued their lives in the basements and cellars of their damaged homes.
April 1995

The Refugees

The Cleansed

He is indubitably mad. Whether he has been driven mad by war, or has always been like this, it is impossible to tell. Sitting on a broken kitchen chair at the side of the road before the village of Domanovici, he cuts a pathetic, gaunt, bearded figure with wild, flashing eyes. Our request for directions simply prompts a hysterical scream. "Go back! Go back!".

Ahead, the hamlet of Aladinići is eerily deserted. The unsurfaced road winds up through the red-roofed, whitewashed houses. In a once neat courtyard to the left of the road a table is overturned, chairs are scattered and, on the ground, the broken dishes still bear the evidence of a hastily abandoned meal. The main door of the house is ajar. The Muslim inhabitants are gone; overtaken by a terrible fate which surely they must have feared in their hearts, but which they hoped and prayed would never actually happen. It is strange how, in war, people always hang on, believing it will never come to *their* door. Too often, they simply leave it too late.

This place has been cleansed like so many other villages in Bosnia. Here, the cleansing has been done by Croats in grim imitation of the process started by their enemies the Serbs last year. A few hundred metres further up the road, the same fate has overtaken the village of Pjesivac. The houses, maybe fifty or sixty, lie empty and the road into the village is blocked by barbed wire, rocks and signs marked 'MINE'.

At the local headquarters of the ICRC and UNHCR in Medjugorje, just half an hour's drive away, they have told us that there is definitely no ethnic cleansing going on around this area between Mostar and Stolac. "It's all over, there are no Muslims left," Claudio Baranzini, head of mission for the ICRC, confidently assures us.

But there are tell-tale signs which suggest otherwise; which suggest that these wretched people have been driven from their homes within the past few days – indeed, if not in the last few hours. A chair on which someone has recently sat in the sun, padded in yellow velvet, sits at the side of the road, the seat dry and unmarked by the rain of previous days. The houses are not yet emptied; the looting process uncompleted; and the newly ripened leaves of the tobacco plants in the fields have been picked at the bottom.

Now there is a group of Croat houses at the side of the road and you fancy that their emerging occupants are looking guiltily on at you. You know, they say that the ethnic Croats of western Herzegovina are more fiercely Croat than even the Croats in Croatia itself. Something for a Muslim to conjure with. In the front passenger seat, our 'guide', a middle-aged unkempt local who speaks some German, seems increasingly uneasy and nervous. His head cranes forward anxiously and his eyes dart from side to side. He is not the only one grown anxious. I realise that we cannot possibly be meant to be seeing this newly created panorama of horror.

I guess that our driver, Erich, the *Tageszeitung* correspondent in Bosnia, is unhappy. He is nervously asking our guide how much further to our appointment. Even the two large and intrepid Finnish lady journalists travelling with us have fallen uncharacteristically silent beside me in the back of the ancient Mercedes. In English, I suggest to Erich that we have to get rid of our guide as we approach the brow of a hill. Below, the road enters the cover of trees and then curves back to the main road we have previously left. He cannot possibly be carrying through his promise to escort us to Vide Milanović, the elusive local army official who handles the press.

Erich stops the car and looks to our guide, who is now sweating profusely. "We go no further," he tells him in German. At this, our guide leaps from the car and bolts up the dirt track towards the brow of the hill. We reverse furiously back.

I am thinking, in this part of Bosnia you can buy a virtually brand new Mercedes for around $1,500. Stolen, of course. Even our battered specimen would command a good five hundred. When the local economy has ceased to exist, robbing strangers of cars, money and sometimes their lives is the last truly profitable activity left.

We were assigned our guide by the military police in Domanovici and I suppose we demonstrated a naive faith in the military uniform. Yes, he would lead us to Milanović, just down the road. And so we pulled away through the road block of concrete and barbed wire, past the military police and the ragtag crew of drunken soldiery sat in front of the local bar. "Just up the road" stretches into kilometres and winds up through village after village newly emptied of their occupants.

Back in Domanovici, the military checkpoint is strangely abandoned; the battered cars painted in camouflage colours are gone; and the bar is deserted, half-emptied glasses still on the tables awaiting the imbibers' return. On the way out, the village idiot seems to stare disbelievingly at us and then his face wreathes in a smile. He raises his hand in a V for victory sign and shouts "Don't come back! Don't come back!"

We are relieved to return to the haven of our most basic of *pensions*. Even Medjugorje seems almost civilised: a curious blend of Las Vegas and Lourdes. It is a modern town made up of a long curling strip of bars, restaurants, casinos and shops selling religious geegaws. Here, on June 26 1981, six children saw a vision of the Virgin Mary preaching a message of peace from a hill and a boom town was born, albeit briefly. Exactly ten years later, to the day, Yugoslavia broke up and war enveloped the Federation. Back in the safety of our *pension*, drinks are called for and over brandies we wonder at all this amoral madness, at the spiral down into vicious anarchy.

Our German conversation attracts two unprepossessing and drunken louts from the next table. Udo, probably about 40 from his accent comes from the German *Ruhrgebiet*. He is a veteran of the French

Peace Be With You. Medjugorje *November 1993*

Foreign Legion and the menacing effect of his filthy camouflage uniform is rounded off by a black bandanna around his skull. He wants to talk. His colleague, Klaus, is not so communicative. Indeed, he does not utter a single word. He is a young boy, 20 years at the most, – with his hair close cropped in the crown style of Germany's neo-Nazis. You can't fail but notice he has hands like hams. They have come to fight in Bosnia. But why?

Certainly not for the money. They earn the equivalent of just a couple of hundred Deutschmarks a month. And, it is evident, not from any spiritual or moral conviction. They make it clear they are here to kill Muslims. But why? Says Udo with a grin. "Es macht mir Spass." *It gives me pleasure.*

In this country gone mad I am driven to thinking the village idiot may be the sanest man in Bosnia.

Refugee from Velika Kladuša at Turanj
August 1994

Opposite: In the spring of 1993 bitter and bloody fighting broke out between Muslim and Croat throughout Bosnia as the former allies turned on each other in the wake of the Vance Owen proposals for 'cantonisation' of the country. Pre-emptive strikes for territory took place from Mostar in the south to the Lašva Valley in the north. This Croat village (*opposite,*) not far from the British UN base at Vitez, was cleansed by Muslim fundamentalist forces in response to Croat cleansing of Muslim villages. The writing on the wall proclaims 'God is great'. *June 1993*

Above: 'Funny Times, Funny Days' says the T-shirt. But this youngster in the refugee camp at Gasinči in Croatia – a former Yugoslav army training camp packed with tented accommodation – has no idea when he might return to his old home or find a new one. The temporary accommodation at Gasinči became a permanent refugee camp holding up to 8,000 refugees from Bosnia at any one time. *June 1992*

In the summer of 1994 bitter fighting broke out between the Bosnian government 5th Korpus and local Muslims in the Bihać enclave, supporters of the local warlord Fikret Abdić. Initially, the government forces gained control of the area around Velika Kladuša and Abdić's supporters were obliged to flee. In a typically confusing set of local alliances, Abdić had obtained the support of Croatian Serbs in the self-styled Serbian Republic of Krajina. The Serbs allowed Abdić supporters to flee across their territory and to set up camp in No Man's Land between their own forces and those of The Republic of Croatia.

And so that summer more than 10,000 displaced people came to the shattered village of Turanj (*opposite*) where they settled in ruined and booby-trapped homes for more than six months. When Abdić and the Serbs recaptured Velika Kladuša they set off back home again … *August 1994*

Twenty-four hour ration pack for six-year-old
Ansa from Novi Travnik, central Bosnia.
June 1993

Mortar attack victims. Two busloads of men, women and children travelling to Tuzla from Austria were mortared as their papers were checked at a Croat roadblock near Novi Travnik in central Bosnia. Several died, many were injured and those able to carry on crowded onto one bus. As night fell, they were stranded outside the British UN base at Vitez. They were not admitted to the base or given any assistance despite their night long pleas. A British army officer implored them, "Please go away. You are bringing this base into danger." *June 1993*

Right: War artist Peter Howson painted the dramatic scene which took place outside the British camp, basing his painting on this photograph (*reproduced courtesy of Flowers East Gallery*).

The charcoal drawing of Paul Harris was made by Peter Howson at Vitez, June 1993.

Improvised barber's shop for refugees from Velika Kladuša.
August 1994

Up to the wire. Sick refugees from Velika Kladuša wait to be transported for
medical treatment to the hospital in Karlovac, Croatia. After treatment they
were returned to their 'homes' in No Man's Land in Turanj. *December 1994*

Breakfast at the refugee centre in Travnik for this
Muslim girl 'ethnically cleansed' from northern
Bosnia. Thousands of refugees were crowded into
the 100 year-old local secondary school –
sometimes sleeping thirty or forty to a room.
November 1992

What future? Mother and daughter, Muslim refugees from Modriča, northern Bosnia, in the refugee camp at Virovitica, Croatia. *April 1993*

Putting it Back Together Again ...

Razim Pesarović and his wife and two children are looking forward to moving out of the henhouse. The village of Rajska, in Bosnia's northern Tuzla region, was invaded by Serb forces early in the War – during May 1992 – and it was not until the following December that Bosnian government forces succeeded in driving them out of the village of some 150 houses. As the Serbs left, they burned the houses with phosphorus bombs and blew up public buildings like the school and the mosque. And so, when Rasim and his family returned they found their house roofless and gutted by fire, and they moved into the henhouse across the yard.

It might seem unlikely that anybody would live in the shell of their house ever again. But Scottish European Aid delivered a lorry load of roofing timber to the Pesarovics, and oak to the local joiner to fashion window and door frames. Later, roof tiles, doors and sufficient timber to floor one room will be delivered and before the winter sets in, the family will move back in. All at a cost of just £2,000, which is considerably less than it costs to sustain a refugee family for a year in unhappy, overcrowded and substandard communal accommodation.

Although the Pesarovics were the first family to benefit in their particular village, elsewhere in the Tuzla region SEA had already successfully pioneered the rebuilding of war damaged homes. In Dobosnica, the renovation of more than 20 homes was well advanced in the summer of 1994 and experience there helped establish the SEA criteria for assistance.

Field director Magnus Wolfe Murray explained these criteria, "In the first instance, villages are identified where locals are already returning to their damaged property and have a clear desire to move back in." Houses suitable for renovation are identified; bills of quantities drawn up; materials ordered and delivered to site by SEA. At this point, SEA hands over to local labour – the beneficiaries are left to get on with the job themselves.

Mr Pesarović explained, "My family, relatives and members of the local community will all help." Throughout former Yugoslavia, manual skills necessary for carrying out building work are readily available: it was quite normal in the days of peace for families and friends to literally build their own homes.

SEA was run then by 25 year-old Magnus Wolfe Murray. He made an unlikely boss for an international aid operation with an annual budget pushing around five million dollars: part restless Bohemian, part harassed executive, large part visionary. The Tuzla office on the outskirts of the city is on the second floor of an industrial building leased from the local refuse disposal company and here more than three dozen local and expatriate employees work: admin staff in the main office, communications technicians in the radio room, water engineers poring over maps and charts, and in a room at the end of the building, two local workers are busy manufacturing a targeted 200,000 candles for next winter. The candle machine was donated by Children in Need, the charity of HRH The Duchess of York, who has taken a strong personal interest in the activities of SEA and helped to raise funds for the Tuzla activities.

The first floor houses a temporary school for refugee children and the yard below bustles with the white and blue-painted 20-truck fleet and Land-rovers of SEA, with a throng of milling children and a collection of stray dogs adopted by SEA operatives in the field. It all seems like, well, chaos. The incredible thing is that it seems to work.

The SEA story is as bizarre and unlikely as its boss. Five years ago, Magnus was an unemployed skateboarder in Glasgow with an unfulfilled, if unarticulated, yearning to do something a little more useful. His elder brother Rupert, who was also involved in founding SEA, was a struggling writer – another brother is a Buddhist monk. A first enterprise, which "involved sticking things into black plastic bags" for Romania, developed into an operation focused on one of the worst orphanages in Moldavia. There, in 1990, they found 120 handicapped and abandoned children without food, medicines or care. Today, it is a model operation acting as a training and resource centre for the whole of the country.

Scottish European Aid truck fleet loaded with water pipes, Tuzla.
June 1994

At the end of 1992 Magnus conducted a study of the requirements in Bosnia and identified the Tuzla region and its decaying and damaged infrastructure as one of the most urgent cases for treatment.

If a simple phrase sums up the philosophy of SEA it is "hands up, not hand outs". It believes in enabling people to help themselves, acting as a catalyst, rather than as some sort of Santa Claus riding in to dish out *largesse* to an increasingly helpless and enfeebled local population.

You can see young Magnus is a source of some amazement locally. Decisions are not usually made around here by youthful dynamos, but rather by corpulent, middle-aged and greying executives schooled in the bureaucratic red tape of Tito's Yugoslavia. But, after more than 18 months out here, it is equally clear that he has become respected and admired, although this does not come without its problems.

The days are filled with politics, negotiation, bureaucracy, seemingly endless cups of Turkish coffee, driving at high speed in battered Landrovers around frontline positions, and organising office, workshop and warehouse. Although much of the best housing stock in Bosnia has been destroyed by the war, the paperwork and the bureaucracy has not been destroyed along with it.

At a meeting with the President of the Lukavac municipality, after an inspection visit to see progress in Dobosnica just a couple of kilometres from the front line, the smoke-filled room at the House of Culture was full of demands and exasperation. "You must make us more houses," urged the President. "You must work in more villages. We need more materials, more help. You can make these things happen. You speak to UNHCR. I will give you my trees for the work."

Magnus listens patiently as the demands mount. It is clear that for these people, Magnus is an accessible representative – maybe the only accessible representative – from an outside world far removed from their knowledge and reality.

"But, my friend, money does not grow on trees," Magnus calmly observes.

"But we will provide the trees. You will tell the world for us – and the money will come." This is certain. This is a demand which cannot be rejected. And now the compliments. "You are like a Bosnian man – you live with us, you are like us, you are speaking our language." This is high praise indeed.

This is not simple flattery. The achievements are, indeed, tangible. The housing renovation scheme is relatively new and SEA has already been responsible for renewing or improving water supplies to more than twenty local communities. In the bitterly contested town of Gradacac, the most northerly point on the government-held front line, the hospital already has a new roof courtesy SEA who provided nails, bitumenized paper, galvanised iron sheeting and plates of plexiglas. With these basic materials, local workers replaced the entire roof in just two weeks, working at night to avoid the daily shelling. In the industrial zone there, a series of tanks, a pumping station and a filter to remove the pollution from the water are under installation to restore water supplies. SEA's water engineers have developed a new concept in water tank design: round, semi-subterranean tanks built for maximum strength and protection in the war zone.

The quality of water in Tuzla itself is seriously deteriorating as repairs to the infrastructure are not carried out and increased demands are placed on it by a population of 135,000 swollen by around 80,000 refugees. SEA's engineers have now devised a scheme to sink new boreholes and lay new pipes from the existing water table. The pipework for this operation will require sixty-five 40-foot articulated trucks to bring in the 36-foot long lengths of pipe on a hazardous two day journey from the coast, through forest and over mountain on roads which are little more than dirt tracks in places. SEA has arranged the finance to buy the hardware involved, has the technical expertise to carry out the operation and last week Magnus was cajoling and harrying the Tuzla authorities into supplying the trucks and the local labour.

There have been serious setbacks from time to time. The most devastating was on the night of September 30, 1993 when three key employees were mown down by a runaway car. Base co-ordinator Nan Owen and water engineer Matthew Stogdon died, and director of operations Mike Mackenzie lay for months, paralysed, in Stoke Mandeville Hospi-tal. For people who had endured and survived the daily risks of the war zone, it was a tragic irony that they should die so near to SEA's offices in the peace of the Croatian port of Split. Fortuitously for SEA, there is no lack of Scots volunteers stepping forward for its Bosnia operation.

For Douglas Skeldon, driving a lorry around frontlines with loads of wood and pipes is "something useful I always wanted to do." Colleague Alistair Lindsay, just 22, from Edinburgh has the reserves of idealism which characterise so many aid workers. "We're doing something worthwhile – working for people rather than profit." And 19 year-old Selma, a local office worker in Tuzla, joined SEA simply because "around here it is the best known and respected aid organisation."

The city of Tuzla itself is one of the most remarkable communities in Europe whose people have stood up, throughout history, for values of pluralism, tolerance and democracy.

During the Second World War the Muslim people of Tuzla succeeded in preventing the destruction of the city's Jewish and Serbian communities by Fascist troops. At the beginning of the present war in former Yugoslavia, Tuzla's non-nationalist municipal authority reacted by putting together a multi-ethnic Citizen's Forum of 10,000 people to resist the politics of ethnic division and keep a normal civic life alive. Despite immense military, practical and political pressures, culminating in the horrific and senseless massacre in May 1995 of nearly eighty young people in the centre of the old town, three years on the municipality is still sustaining these values. This is in no small measure due to the tireless efforts of Tuzla's mayor, Selim Bešlagić, whose achievements have received recognition worldwide.

Tuzla's struggle, and Bosnia's struggle, is our struggle. It is the struggle of the whole of Europe for peace, democracy, cultural diversity and tolerance against the evil forces of Fascism.

That is why we must make a stand.

The industrial city of Tuzla, and the region around, has managed to retain its
multi-ethnic character and identity probably more successfully than any other
part of Bosnia. Its location, in the very north of Bosnia, is relatively remote
from the capital or central Bosnia: seven hours or so drive over appalling roads.

June 1994

Shortages – not least of petrol – are everywhere in the Tuzla region and the
horse and cart have made a comeback as a convenient form of transport.
June 1994

The charity Scottish European Aid has made a significant impact in the Tuzla region. Taking aid well beyond the concept of the food parcel, SEA has worked on infrastructure projects such as restoring water pipes, pumping stations and re-roofing houses. Generally, SEA supply the materials to people anxious to return to their homes and they then carry out the work themselves. "Hands up, not hand outs," as their field director Magnus Wolfe Murray put it.

Above: House undergoing re-roofing at Dobosnica.

Top right: The Pesarovics receive building materials from SEA to repair their house.

Right: This house was deliberately destroyed with a phosphorus bomb by retreating Serbs. *June 1994*

Journalists at work on the frontline.

Right: The medieval castle, Gradacac, on the northern frontline of the Tuzla region.
June 1994

Left: War art from the heart. Almira is a self-taught artist from the town of Gradacac who discovered her own way of expressing her anger and emotion. Her deeply disturbing images of war were exhibited at the Bologna Book Fair in Italy and have been published as posters. An extraordinary phenomenon of the war in Bosnia is how people who would not regard themselves as artists have turned to literature, music and painting as a release from its dark pressures. *June 1994*

Above: Magnus Wolfe Murray, then field director of Scottish European Aid, in the project's joinery workshop, Dobosnica. *June 1994*

A small boy outside his ruined home in the village of Dobosnica, near Tuzla. It was subsequently re-roofed by SEA.

June 1994

The Minutes of Hasiba

from an interview on 6 November 1992

They came at night with their flashlights
Through PARTISANS' HALL
They took me with them and we drove
To a bridge over the Drina
On the bridge stood
Ten older women Tied up
And fifteen soldiers They yelled
Here comes one of yours See how we love her
Then they did everything to me All fifteen of them
Afterwards they smoked and put out their cigarettes
In my hair Then one soldier took
His knife and slit a farmer's throat
Not quite through So that his head stayed on his shoulders
It didn't bother me anymore I had
Seen so much already I didn't care
Then he tore his head off entirely and they played
Soccer with it and laughed and laughed
I knew the farmers They were
Neighbours colleagues relatives
Just a few weeks ago I knew most
Of the soldiers too They were
Neighbours colleagues relatives They were
Men like you

Holger Teschke, translated by
Margitt Lehbert

White-out

Blindingly from the east blizzards come.
The first flakes sizzle on the stove,
as the storm gathers momentum.
Were we in such a land, my love …

It is of you we think, children of Bosnia,
your ghosts like white birds passing
over, passing over: so that already
the sky is black with your wings.

Stewart Conn

In the summer of 1995 the so-called UN-declared 'safe-haven' of Srebrenica in
eastern Bosnia was allowed to fall to advancing Serb forces. Some 30,000 inhabitants
of the enclave were ethnically cleansed. Most of the men were taken prisoner and an
untold number were killed. Additionally, many younger women were abducted,
raped and murdered. Only women, children and the most elderly of men were
allowed by the Serbs to make their way to safety: bused to the confrontation lines
near to Kladanj and then forced to make their way across no-man's land. Once in
government-held territory they were transferred to an improvised refugee camp on
the UN base at Tuzla Airport. At its peak, it held more than 19,700 refugees. Said
US Rangers Major Guy Sands of the Serbs at Tuzla air base, "I cannot believe the
inhumanity of these people – I cannot even call them people – who did this to
women and children and old men. This is the new genocide." *July 1995*

144   Refugee from Srebrenica *July 1995*